ARDENT COMPLAINTS AND EQUIVOCAL PIETY

The Portrayal Of The Crusader In Medieval German Poetry

William E. Jackson

Copyright © 2003 by
University Press of America,® Inc.
4501 Forbes Boulevard
Suite 200
Lanham, Maryland 20706
UPA Acquisitions Department (301) 459-3366

PO Box 317
Oxford
OX2 9RU, UK

Library of Congress Control Number: 2003110873
ISBN 0-7618-2550-9 (paperback : alk. ppr.)

Contents

iv

Preface

This book has what I would term a prehistory. In 1981, I brought with me to the University of Virginia a manuscript in progress, in German, with the working title *Reinmar und die Kreuzzugsdichtung* in which I was attempting a reassessment of medieval German crusade poetry from the point of view of one of it's authors. The project was shelved while I embarked on a fifteen-year stint in the administration of a research institute. I did manage to rework what I considered the core of the project and publish it in the journal *Germanisch-romanische Monatsschrift* (1993) under the title "Das Kreuzzugmotiv in Reinmars Lyrik." Otherwise, the project was in jeopardy of abandonment since rather heavy administrative duties only permitted the publication of an article here and there.

Then, in the fall of 1994, I taught a graduate course on the crusades. To the five students who took that course—Anthony Aue, James Black, Marta Hanewald, Annette Uhlenkott, and Patricia Underwood—I owe the inspirational spark that stirred up my desire to give another try at writing a book on the crusades that would be in some sense a continuation of the original project, but would be in many ways a quite different book. The new focus on German crusade poetry as a reflection of contemporary developments in European culture, for instance, probably owes something to my days in research administration, and specifically to the reading of applications from various academic disciplines employing various methodologies. However, I could not be more pleased that this book is essentially an outgrowth of a course which was well received and which was a joy to teach.

Desire became decision when I left the research institute in 1996. I am very grateful to Professor Raymond J. Nelson, then Dean of the Faculty of Arts and Sciences at the University of Virginia for the year of leave in which the bulk of the first draft of this book was written. A three-year stint as chair of my department delayed things a bit, but may also have worked out to the good of the project by forcing, after each interruption, a healthy reconsideration of various aspects of the discussion.

It is my pleasure to thank the University Press of America for its handling of this project and particularly Mr. Steven Ryan and Ms. Beverly Baum for their patience and continued helpfulness. Special thanks also to Ms. Mary F. Rose, who solved numerous technological problems for me, Ms. Valerie Redd, who completed the camera-ready copy, and Ms. Melody Palmer who guided me through the indexing.

The responsibility for whatever is lacking in the project is, of course, my own.

Charlottesville, Virginia   June 10, 2002

Abbreviations

BGDSL	=	*Beiträge zur Geschichte der deutschen Sprache und Literatur.*
DMA	=	*Dictionary of the Middle Ages.* Ed. Joseph R. Strayer. 13 vols. New York: Scribner, 1982-1989.
DVLG	=	*Deutsche Vierteljahresschrift für Literatur wissenschaft und Geistesgeschichte.*
GAG	=	*Göppinger Arbeiten zur Germanistik.*
GR	=	*Germanic Review.*
GRM	=	*Germanisch-romanische Monattschrift.*
JEGP	=	*Journal of English and Germanic Philology.*
KD	=	ULrich Müller, ed. *Kreuzzugsdichtung.*
KLD	=	Carl von Kraus, ed. *Deutsche Liederdichter.*
MF	=	*Des Minnesangs Frühling.* Ed. Hugo Moser and Helmut Tervooren. 33rd ed. 2 vols. Stuttgart: Hirzel, 1977.
MLR	=	*Modern Language Review.*
NM	=	*Neuphilologische Mitteilungen.*
OGS	=	*Oxford German Studies.*
PS&Q	=	*Philologische Studien und Quellen.*

VL^2	=	Kurt Ruh, ed. *Die deutsche Literatur des Mittelalters: Verfasserlexikon.* 2nd edition.
ZDA	=	*Zeitschrift für deutsches Altertum und deutsche Literatur.*
ZDP	=	*Zeitschrift für deutsche Philologie.*

General Introduction

I. Problems and Issues

This main focus of this study is a group of medieval German poems portraying the crusader facing battle. In most of the poems, the crusader is about to depart for duty, but in a few he is either underway or already in the military arena. In every case, the crusade commitment has resulted in discomfort, and in most the crusader views his situation with patent distress.

The earliest of these poems can be dated around the time of the Third Crusade (1189-1190) while the latest were probably composed during the first half of the thirteenth century. The authors of the poems, in roughly chronological order, are Friedrich von Hausen, Hartmann von Aue, Albrecht von Johansdorf, Reinmar der Alte, Otto von Botenlauben, Friedrich von Leiningen, and Der Burggraf von Lienz. The first named, Friedrich von Hausen, was a crusader whose participation is a matter of historical record: Hausen took part in the Third Crusade from which he did not return. For the other authors no such record exists.

Several of these authors--namely Johansdorf, Botenlauben, Leiningen, and Lienz--also composed poems featuring the portrayal of a woman whom the crusader is about to leave behind. In two cases (Johansdorf and Leiningen), crusader and beloved woman engage in dialogue about his departure. The remaining cases will turn out to be more complicated. However, in all cases the woman is portrayed as being perturbed and annoyed at the ensuing separation. Hence the role of the woman complements the portrayal of the crusader in an interesting way.

This study also includes discussion of poems portraying persons who are intensely interested or very involved in a crusade without a clear indication whether the person in question is actually a crusader. The composers of these poems are Heinrich von Rugge, Neidhart, and Rubin. As opposed to the poems of the previously mentioned group of poets, where a crusader clearly faces military duty, here in the poems of Rugge, Neidhart, and Rubin such a duty is not a certainty. In Rugge's poems we encounter a man who is fervently interested in crusade recruitment, but we will hear a number of indications that he may himself not be answering the call. Neidhart, on the other hand, portrays a man somewhere in the battle zone who decries the terrible conditions faced by a crusading army, but without clearly indicating whether or not he is a member of the army whose discomforts he is witnessing and sharing. In Rubin's case, finally, we will again hear pro-crusade sentiment, as in the case of Rugge, but we will also hear reasons to doubt whether this sentiment amounts to a commitment to military action.

Within these three groups of poems we shall encounter a considerable variety and range of reactions to various aspects of the crusades. The poems that portray the crusader dwell almost exclusively on his pain of parting from home, on his concern about loved ones left behind—especially the beloved woman—and, in a few cases, on the desire to return home. The crusading obligation is pictured in these poems as the occasion for ardent complaints, for laments about the need to part, and for dwelling, often at some length, on the painful distress caused by the inner conflict between duty and inclination.

In the crusade poems portraying the woman, with the interesting exception of one poem by Rubin, instead of indirect complaints about the burdens of the crusade obligation we hear direct declarations of **outspoken opposition** to the crusade per se. In fact, while there are several German crusade poems which feature a male persona calling on the woman to support her man in his crusading obligation and even--as we shall hear in a poem by Hartmann von Aue--to urge him on his way and pray for him, to my knowledge there exists no medieval poem in any language in which a female persona is portrayed as speaking out in support of crusading. With Rubin as the exception, the voice of woman is used by male poets in German poetry

PART I.
Portraying The Crusader In Medieval German Poetry

and, as we shall hear later, in other vernacular traditions, exclusively to express vehement complaints againsts the crusades.

Curiously underrepresented in the crusade poems of all these authors are reflections of the crusade as warfare. The "pagan" enemy and the battles against them, for example, are all but invisible, in stark contrast to crusade poetry in Latin, from which we will hear shortly. In Neidhart's '*Ez gruonet wol diu heide*' (below, Part III), we will hear the speaker refer in one brief line to the miserable state of a crusading army, but the only group named in the poem is not one of enemies, but allies ("die Walhen"). By contrast, a number of the Latin poems dwell at length on military persons and places of military events, often identifying them with proper names. Meanwhile, the German poems portraying the crusader all but exclude any reference to the impending confrontation with the realities of warfare, while focusing almost exclusively on ardent complaints about concerns at home. There is therefore much about these poems that is far from self-evident.

II. A Brief Look at Scholarship

This study will show that Middle High German lyric poetry of the crusades, that is, the crusade poetry of the German-speaking laity of the later 12th and 13th centuries, is at base a poetry of inner struggle, misgivings, and disenchantment about the crusades, and, in a few cases, outright rejection of that undertaking. During the history of scholarship on this poetry, the traces of such sentiments have been noted, but consistently either downplayed, ignored, or explained away.

In an influential article from the year 1886, G(eorg) Wolfram makes the claim that the German crusade songs of the 12th and 13th centuries are based almost completely on the crusade sermons and papal bulls of that time.[1] In the same article, Wolfram makes the additional claim that the German crusade poems in question are limited in their content to four basic thoughts, namely: 1) God has suffered for us; 2) we must repay him for this; 3) our sins also demand retribution; and 4) we earn by our service eternal salvation.[2]

Both these claims are problematic and actually misleading. The tension between the claims themselves and the texts upon which Wolfram purports to base them becomes evident immediately in his own article when he turns to a discussion of Friedrich von Hausen. As already indicated, Hausen will be discussed below as the earliest known German crusade poet and possibly the first of all. We have also heard already that Hausen is historically attested as a crusader who died in

1190 on the Third Crusade. Wolfram notes that Hausen's thoughts about the crusades are so wound up in his love poetry that he offers little that is useful for the purposes of Wolfram's article.[3] Thus, by Wolfram's own admission, the poems of Hausen do not fit his description of crusade poetry as based almost fully on sermons. Hausen's poems also do not confine themselves to Wolfram's four listed categories of subject matter, and indeed, as we shall hear later in our discussion, actually excludes them. We shall also learn that Friedrich von Hausen is by no means an exception in this regard among crusade poets. A number of the crusader portrayals by other poets which we shall encounter below, like those of Hausen, do not contain even a hint of Wolfram's four categories of content.

Unfortunately, Wolfram's article, as problematic as it is, has exercised considerable influence on subsequent scholarship. Medieval German crusade poetry has continued to be interpreted as poetry based on and formulated in support of crusade ideology as found in sermons and bulls. Wolfram also established an unfortunate model by summarizing the supposed contents of this poetry before discussing the poems in question, and then failing to note the discrepancy between his summary and the actual contents of the poems under discussion.

Not quite eighty years later, Wolfram's summary was reproduced verbatim by Maria Böhmer in her book on German crusade poetry.[4] Böhmer also follows Wolfram's lead in failing to do justice to the texts of the poems that she discusses. She does note, as Wolfram did not, that medieval German poetry was composed in an age when both the idea and the reality of the crusades were under attack from vocal opponents.[5] However, she insists that, as far as German crusade poetry was concerned, that criticism was secondary.[6] German crusade poetry, Böhmer maintains, was remarkably unified in its pure crusade enthusiasm ("merkwürdig einheitlich im Ausdruck der reinen Kreuzzugsbegeisterung"), and she adds that this should not surprise us since the function of that poetry was the inner strengthening of knightly consciousness ("die innere Festigung des Ritterbewußtseins").[7] In point of fact, we shall learn that precisely such sentiments as pure crusade enthusiasm and such ambitions as the inner strengthening of knightly consciousness are to be found in only a very few German crusade poems, and mainly in those of Rugge and Rubin. The poems portraying the crusader are dominated by the kind of disenchantment with the crusades and somber outlooks that seem more likely to weaken knightly consciousness than to strengthen it.

Three years after the appearance of Wolfram's article in 1886, another article was published, by Hermann Schindler, which has had a similar unfortunate influence on scholarship of a later date.[8] Schindler departs from Wolfram and anticipates Böhmer in duly noting the presence and spread of antipathy to the crusades during the period in question. Unfortunately, however, he also anticipates Böhmer in denying any evidence of anti-crusade sentiment in German crusade poetry before the appearance of the thirteenth-century poet Neidhart.[9] Schindler's touting of Neidhart as the innovator of anti-crusade sentiment among German poets, a view that we shall find to be mistaken, has found agreement in an article by Ursula Schulze which appeared about ninety years after Schindler's publication and roughly a decade after Böhmer's.

Like Schindler, Schulze pictures Neidhart as the sole and initial creator of an implicit anti-crusade poetry ("ein implizites Antikreuzzugsgedicht").[10] It is unclear why Schulze characterizes Neidhart's anti-crusade sentiment as implicit, given the bitterness of the strongly worded attack on the crusades which we shall hear below in Neidhart's own words. In any case, while noting in passing the possibility of counter-positions ("Gegenpositionen") in crusade poetry of the 12th century, that is, poetry preceding Neidhart, Schulze still insists, like Böhmer, that these counter-positions could not seriously detract from the encompassing character of crusade enthusiasm ("der übergreifende Charakter der Kreuzzugsbegeisterung").[11] Thus Schulze also sees a dominance of pro-crusade sentiment in German poetry before Neidhart. She explains Neidhart's allegedly innovative anti-crusade stance as resulting from a rash of mishaps and disturbing events transpiring in Neidhart's own day.[12] Schulze apparently sees no need to discuss the stance of poets before Neidhart; she explicitly mentions only Hartmann von Aue and (Neidhart's contemporary) Walther von der Vogelweide.[13] For the other poets before Neidhart, pro-crusade sentiment seems to be simply assumed. In fact, however, we shall hear below that disenchantment with the crusades is a widely expressed sentiment in the poems of Neidhart's twelfth-century predecessors composing in German, while pro-crusade sentiment is much less apparent.

In sum, the texts that constitute the focus of the present study have been treated over a long period of time from a summarily inaccurate point of view. In the process, the false idea has been spread and perpetuated that medieval German crusade poetry composed before the thirteenth century is overwhelmingly, if not exclusively, pro-crusade poetry, that is, poetry of enthusiastic support for the Holy Cause.

A bit of a different case is the study from the year 1980 of Peter Hölzle on 12th-century German and Occitan crusade poetry. In this study, Hölzle sets out to subject to a rigorous examination expressly the kinds of facile assumptions that have dominated the scholarship tradition just summarized.[14] Hölzle notes the presence of numerous passages in German poetry where one hears expressions of misgiving and disenchantment concerning the crusades and even opposition to them.[15] However, he proceeds to disqualify the poems that include such troublesome passages, insisting that they are not actually crusade poems at all in the strict sense of the term. The definition of crusade poetry by which Hölzle judges the poems of his study is remarkable for its stringency. According to this definition, namely, crusade poems are limited to those which express in most of their stanzas or lines a summons to involvement in the crusades, often in response to crusade sermons.[16] This definition, Hölzle adds immediately, is valid not only for Occitan and German crusade poetry, which he treats in his book, but also for French and Latin crusade poetry, which he does not.

Hölzle's definition may remind readers of Wolfram's above-quoted statement equating the contents of the German crusade poems of the 12th and 13th centuries to that of crusade sermons and papal bulls. Readers may also remember that this statement by Wolfram caused difficulty in his own article when he began discussing the texts of the poems in question. The case is similar with Hölzle's definition covering essentially the same poems (and their Occitan counterparts), except that the difficulties in Hölzle's case are considerably greater. Of the roughly twenty-five German poems discussed by Hölzle, which had prior to his study been called crusade poems, only **six** meet the qualifications required by his definition. Furthermore, the excluded poems include some of the best known German poems otherwise known as crusade songs. In fact, among these non-qualifying poems is found surely the most famous of all, namely: the poem '*Mîn herze und mîn lîp diu wellent scheiden*' by the historically attested crusader Friedrich von Hausen (below, Part I). Hausen's poem qualifies for Hölzle **merely** as one of the songs with crusade connection ("Lieder mit Kreuzzugsbezug").[17]

Thus the same Friedrich von Hausen whose preoccupation with love rendered him an unsatisfactory subject for Wolfram in the 1880's is also a vexing case for Hölzle in 1980. Wolfram avoided further difficulty by quickly dropping Hausen from his discussion. Hölzle can take no such easy way out, having committed himself to discussing the poets represented in his study in some detail. Hölzle, again like Wolfram, has to admit rather soon that Hausen does not fit his definition. Hausen's audience, Hölzle tells us, must have experienced discomfort at recognizing ("beklemmende Erkenntnis") that Hausen's poetry, in comparison with clerical crusade propaganda, sounds like latent crusade criticism.[18] With this admission, Hölzle anticipates a major claim of the present study. A little later, Hölzle is heard to remark further that, for a model crusader, Hausen betrays a disturbingly detached attitude toward the crusade.[19] Unfortunately, these jaundiced observations do not cause Hölzle to go back and reconsider the main argument(s) of his book. Neither, I might add, do his similar observations about fellow poets of Hausen, treated in Hölzle's study and the present one, whose texts, as will be noted below, are similarly bothersome.

Still, Hölzle's observations on individual poems and poets, though mustered in support of a thesis which simply does not stand up to scrutiny, are consistently well formulated and have proven very useful to me in support of an opposing view. For, in fact, contrary to Hölzle's thesis, German crusade poetry in which the crusader is portrayed does not consist of propaganda, and rarely contains expressions of pro-crusade enthusiasm. Rather it features prominently the very kinds of ardent complaints and equivocal piety that raised Hölzle's suspicions about model crusader Friedrich von Hausen. These suspicions were in fact all too well taken and it is unfortunate that Hölzle's reaction to them was to blame Hausen for not being what Hölzle's stringent propaganda thesis needed him to be.

III. Procedure and Outline

This introduction will be followed by a brief treatment of Latin crusade poetry. This opening discussion, which I call a prologue, will be essentially an exercise in benchmarking. It is in Latin crusade poetry, namely, that one finds expressed the strong and clearly articulated support of the crusades that scholars have repeatedly expected and claimed to find in medieval German poems despite indications to the contrary. Furthermore, despite the small number of

Latin crusade poems that have been preserved, it is clear that there was at least one dramatic change in the historical development of this poetry. This change, which was triggered by what was probably **the** major turning point in the history of the crusades, namely the Battle of Hattin in 1187, coincides very closely with the composition of the earliest extant crusade poems in German.

The Latin prologue will be followed by three sections, each focusing on one of the three groups of medieval German crusade poems indicated above, namely: poems portraying crusaders; poems featuring a female persona; and poems by Rugge, Neidhart, and Rubin portraying speakers of uncertain status. For the German poems, the extant Latin crusade poems composed before the Battle of Hattin will mainly serve to provide contextualization by contrast: motifs and features which scholars have sought in medieval German crusade poetry with rare success will turn out to be characteristic of the Latin poetry of that earlier era. The Latin crusade poems composed after the Battle of Hattin will themselves differ starkly from the pre-Hattin Latin poems. It will be interesting to see how many features of Latin crusade poetry composed before Hattin differ from features shared by Latin crusade poetry after Hattin and the crusade poetry in vernacular Middle High German. With the early Latin poems as a point of contrast for both, comparisons between the contemporaneous developments after 1187 of poetry composed in Latin, the language of the clerical world, and in Middle High German, the language of the German-speaking laity, promise to be uniquely intriguing. Leaving aside the possibililty of lost and unknown texts, the extant poems in both these developments also cover roughly the same time period, waning noticeably in both the Latin and Middle High German traditions before the mid-thirteenth century, while the crusades themselves continued on for some time.

The three groups of Middle High German poems will be treated in the order mentioned. This order seems to correspond to some degree with their probable chronology. The poems clearly portraying a crusader and which in one case we know to have been authored by one, are concentrated, with few exceptions, in the twelfth century. This seems to be true as well of the poems portraying a female persona, although these are so few in number that it is difficult to speak of a concentration. Of the three poets who composed poems portraying a speaker of uncertain status, one, Heinrich von Rugge belongs to the twelfth century; Neidhart and Rubin belong to the thirteenth.

Prologue: Medieval Latin Crusade Poetry As Background

The Battle of Hattin (July 4, 1887) between the Islamic forces of Saladin and the coalition of forces defending the Kingdom of Jerusalem was possibly the single great turning point in the history of the crusading era. It was also a major turning point in the history of Latin crusade poetry, and indeed in ways that are of considerable importance for the purposes of the present discussion.

The establishment of the Kingdom of Jerusalem had resulted from the only successful crusade, the First Crusade of 1098-1099.[20] From the roughly nine decades between this crusade and the Battle of Hattin there have been preserved nine Latin crusade poems. These belong to a total of twenty-nine poems that have been published in an edition by Goswin Spreckelmeyer. I shall refer to these poems by the numbers in this edition.[21] In his earlier study of Latin crusade poetry, to which I shall also be referring, Spreckelmeyer uses the same numbering system, but assigns to some of the poems a different number.[22]

The twenty extant Latin crusade poems composed after the Battle of Hattin are roughly contemporary with the medieval German crusade poems which are the focus of the present study. The nine Latin crusade poems composed before that battle are important to us mainly because they stand in stark contrast to both the Latin and German poems of the post-Hattin period.

A final section will attempt to place medieval German crusade poetry, along with Latin poetry and a few Romance poems which we will encounter as (possible) models of the German, in the wider context of medieval culture in the late 12th and earlier 13th centuries. We shall learn that disenchantment with the crusades was being expressed in medieval German poetry during an age of wide-spread discomfort with the crusades in European society at large, including church circles.

All translations, unless otherwise identified, are my own. They are provided (only) to facilitate examination of my textual interpretations and are thus intended to convey the original texts as closely as possible.

For one thing, the Latin crusade poems composed after Hattin and the German crusade poems contemporary with them are predominantly somber and plaintive, and in some cases morose and despondent, while the nine Latin poems composed before Hattin exude positive tones that range from confidence to elation. Two examples of the latter are *'Ierusalem, laetare'* (KL 2) and *'Exsultant agmina'* (KL 3), both of which feature verbs of exultation in the first line. *'Ierusalem, laetare'*, which celebrates the crusaders' conquest of Jerusalem in 1099, rejoices in various aspects of that takeover, including the slaughter of the inhabitants and the flowing of their blood in the streets. *'Ierusalem, laetare'* and *'Exsultent agmina'* both celebrate the reversal in power relations in the area: Jerusalem, once the servant of enemy powers, in now their lord. *'Exsultant agmina'* dwells on this significant fact by enumerating the peoples--both friendly and hostile--who have now become Jerusalem's subjects and tributaries.

A good example of confidence is heard in Marbod of Rennes' comparatively short poem *'In toto mundo'* (KL 4) in praise of Bohemond of Taranto, the first European ruler of Antioch; another is heard in a very brief anonymous poem *'Imperator rex Grecorum'* (KL 8) in praise of the emperor of Constantinopel.[23] In both poems the Turks are named as one of several specified peoples who pose no threat to the respective impervious hero of the crusading cause. Perhaps even more impressive is the confidence heard in the earliest poem in this group, *'Ierusalem mirabilis'* (KL 1) composed before the arrival of the crusaders in the Holy Land. Five of the first six stanzas present a sketch of Christ's life and passion which, as Spreckelmeyer points out, has reminded some scholars of Walther von der Vogelweide's famous Palestine poem *'Allerêrst lebe ich mir werde.'* [24] The task at hand, the projected conquest of the Saracens, is a small matter requiring only the four lines of stanza 7:

> Illuc debemus pergere,
> Nostros honores vendere,
> Templum Dei acquirere,
> Saracenos destruere.

> [We ought to go there,
> Wager our honor,
> Take over the temple of God,
> And destroy the Saracens.25]

'Ierusalem, civitas inclita' (KL 9) was composed in the same summer as Saladin's invasion of Syria (1187).[26] In the meantime, the fall of Edessa and the disastrous Second Crusade to which it led,[27] had shown sufficiently that victory was not self-evident. Nevertheless, the poem still expresses full confidence of victory. In fact, in words that rival the lines just quoted from KL 1, the closing stanza of KL 9 proclaims the following assurance of triumph:

Preliemur hic Dei prelia!
Muneremur illic in patria,
Ubi dantur bona stipendia
Militibus, et vera gaudia.

[Let us fight here the fight of God!
We will be rewarded there in our homeland,
Where soldiers will receive
Good rewards and true joy.]

However, the twenty-four preceding stanzas of this somewhat longish poem place these confident tones in an interesting light. For one thing there is sharply worded recognition of invasion by a dangerous enemy host (stanzas 9 and 10). Then there is the extended and shrill call to arms including, in stanza 23, an explicit call to clerics ("Non excusetur clericus") as well as to all classes and ages![28] Every able body is needed in arms for this dire conflict. Finally, there is the revealing emphasis on rewards in the heavenly home: the prospect of this battle includes the explicit anticipation of Christian losses.

The first extant Latin crusade poem composed after the Battle of Hattin is *'Iuxta trenos Ieremie'* (KL 10). It is transmitted in the chronicle of Roger of Hoveden where it is attributed to "quidam clericus dictus Berterus Aurelianensis."[29] In this poem we encounter just about all of the motifs that will dominate Latin crusade poetry from this point on. It begins with the mentioning in the first line of the biblical Jeremiah, one of the major Old Testament prophets and author of the Book of Lamentations where he bemoans the defeat and captivity of the southern Israeli kingdom of Judah. *'Iuxta trenos Ieremie'* introduces a series of poems which will constitute, literally, one almost unbroken jeremiad filled with quotes, allusions, and paraphrases evoking the prophet Jeremiah and his book of Lamentations. The evocation of the solitary, weeping Jerusalem, taken over in the first stanza of KL 10 from the Lamentations of Jeremiah 1: 1,2 (along with

the prophet's name), is also, at least in part, the inspiration for the opening lines of KL 12 (*'Plange, Sion et Judeae'*), 14 (*'Jerusalem, luge'*), 15 (*'Indue cilicium'*), and 22 (*'Sede, sion, in pulvere'*). *'Iuxta trenos Ieremie'* (KL 10) also initiates the tendency to depict the crusades, which the pre-Hattin poems had presented emphatically as a military undertaking, from now on as a spiritual matter: instead of relishing or celebrating the slaughter and domination of the enemy as before, the challenge to the crusader in KL 10 and beyond is the demand for inner spiritual change. As Spreckelmeyer puts it in reference to KL 10, complete submission in faith is now more important for the crusader than military preparation for the trip.[30] Similarly in *'Heu, voce flebili'* (KL 11), which reports in considerable and graphic detail the annihilation of the Christian army by Saladin, Spreckelmeyer notes that, surprisingly, there is no call for participation in an expedition to avenge the defeat. Instead, the poet, probably a German according to Spreckelmeyer, calls for tears as a sign of repentance ("Tränen als Zeichen der Umkehr") and for a conciliatory encounter with God ("eine versöhnende Begegnung mit Gott").[31]

In the Latin crusade poems composed before Hattin the pragmatics of war and the glorification of crusader victories and victors at times relegate God to a minor role. Spreckelmeyer notes that God is not addressed directly in KL 1, *'Ierusalem mirabilis,'* since the paltry matter of defeating the Saracens apparently does not require divine attention; that God is overshadowed in KL 4, *'In toto mundo,'* by the glorious hero Bohemond of Taranto; that God is not mentioned at all in KL 7, *'Exsurgat gens Christiana,'* where the poet has only war talk for the martial nations of Europe; and that in KL 8, *'Imperator rex Grecorum,'* God is upstaged by war itself.[32]

In those Latin crusade poems composed after Hattin, however, matters are essentially reversed: as Spreckelmeyer points out explicitly in regard to KL 16, *'Quod spiritu David precinuit,'* now it is suddenly the war that fades into the background.[33] Spreckelmeyer notes that war as a human encounter is not mentioned either in KL 20, *'Miror, cur tepeat'* or in KL 23, *'Tonat evangelica,'* nor explicitly either in KL 24, *"Crux ego rapta queror'* or KL 26, *'Homo, cur properas.'*[34] Now suddenly it is God's turn to be the dominant center of attention, for now the dire situation in the Holy Land has become God's matter. To be sure, a few poems picture even God as in trouble and distress in the wake of Hattin: KL 13, *'Crucifigat omnes'* issues the call to all who wear the sign of the cross ("quisquis es signatus/ fidei caractere," 3, 1-

2) to be merciful and sad in their hearts for the woes of Christ ("miserans intuere/ corde triste/ damnum Christi," 3,6-7), while the apparently fragmentary KL 17, '*Venit Jesus in propria,*' reports that God has been expelled from his "patrimonia" by "(p)erversae gentes" who have opened the Salomonic temple to the worship of foreign gods ("diis alienis").[35] KL 16, '*Quod spiritu David precinuit,*' proclaims, on the other hand, that God is quite capable of destroying the enemy and freeing his land without crusader assistance ("absque nobis," 5,5-6), a claim, taken over from St. Bernhard of Clairvaux,[36] which we shall hear used in a very interesting way by Albrecht von Johansdorf.

This claim of God's omnipotence requires that defeat be explained, and the standard explanation soon became the sins of the Christians, "peccatis nostris exigentibus"[37] and the resulting need for repentance. This explanation is the basis, for example, of KL 11, '*Heu, voce flebili,*' the poem dated by Spreckelmeyer in early 1188[38] and containing the previously mentioned description of Saladin's victory and the accompanying call to repentance. In the same poem God is made the originator of the Christian defeat, having turned them over to a cruel people ("tradidisse legitur populo crudeli," 23,4) because of their sins.[39] In KL 24, '*Crux ego rapta queror,*' by Galfred of Vinosalvo, the personified and captured Cross explains its situation by proclaiming that it actually allowed itself to be taken because of the sins of the Christians: "Quia tot tua crimina vidi/ Rapta rapi volui" (9-10).

To be sure, the assumption that the victory of the Saracens presupposed the purposeful permission of the Christian God (or His Cross) did not prove universally satisfying to Latin poets in the wake of Hattin and the attendant fall of Jerusalem. KL 12, '*Plange, Sion et Iudeae,*' is mild but pointed in its questioning of God in the midst of a prayer to Him to cease from his anger "cesset ira" (8,1); for if He continues to be harsh, who then will tell of the wonders of Christ ("Quis narrabit Christi mira?" 8,4)? In KL 15, '*Indue cilicium,*' by the poet Erbo, of whom we know only the name, the dissatisfaction with God is expressed a bit more strongly. Spreckelmeyer sees it as precautionary that Erbo couches his pointed criticism of God within a dispute between "Rex Christe" and the distancing third person "homo" (17-18): if King Christ were judged by "humanum iudicium" (17)--here we hear an idea reminiscent of Job 23:1-7--, one could understandably ask some hard questions about His handling of matters in the Holy Land.[40] Among other things, one could wonder about His allowing the

Prince of Darkness (= Satan or Saladin or both?) to lay hands on the saints who, after all, were His lights in this part of the world ("tibi lux fuerant," 22). And on it goes with "homo" raising issue after issue that prevent him from understanding God (33, 37f, 41, etc.). Does God not care? Can He no longer be trusted?[41]

Similar questioning is to be heard in KL 25, *'Diro satis percussus vulnere"*, by Richard of San Germano. Composed after the Christian loss of Damietta in Egypt (1221), the utterances of exasperation are directed to "Iesu bone" (4,1) and coupled with an attack on Rome, "caput et mater omnium" (6,3). Latin crusade poetry thus also knows ardent complaints (and equivocal piety?) of its own. In all these poems, the poets stop short of the absolute rejection of crusading expressed in KL 29, *'Ire si vis ad sermonem,'* with its warning to beware of crusade sermonizing, and they even manage to come up with at least an expression or two that could sound like faith. Nevertheless, their displeasure with God's recent crusading record is more than evident.

It should perhaps be noted for the record that there are poems composed after Hattin that support crusading. In fact, however, among the poems that have survived, these are few in number and are in every case a bit unusual. KL 14, *'Jerusalem, luge,'* is the longest Latin crusade song among those extant. In this poem also, the ultimate reason for the defeat of the Christians and the capture of Jerusalem is the anger of God and not the might of the enemy (51f). However, while *'Jerusalem, luge'* begins with the now familiar plaintive address to the forlorn Jerusalem, it becomes clear very soon that the poet's main interest is Gallia, the district of Europe that had the most substantial linkage with the (crusader) Kingdom of Jerusalem. It is Gallia that has allowed its former glory to wane in the face of unworthy enemies (15-21). It is Gallia that has had to suffer betrayal at the hands of "fraude nocens Constantinopolis exlex" (25). In Spreckelmeyer's judgment, Gallia is viewed in this poem as more important than the Holy Land, and the crusades as a kind of national challenge.[42]

In KL 21, *'Christiani nominis,'* is heard the most clearly and strongly worded call to a crusade in Latin crusade poetry after Hattin. Spreckelmeyer dates this poem cautiously in the period of the Third Crusade and sees it as vehicle of papal propaganda ("Sprachrohr der päpstlichen Propaganda").[43] Making a strong call for crusade participation after Hattin was obviously no easy matter, and this poem clearly shows the strain and pressure. Spreckelmeyer notes a marked

similarity to a pre-Hattin poem, namely KL 4, *'In toto mundo'* by Marbod of Rennes. As there, here in KL 21 also there is a call for a cessation of conflict among Christians,[44] a matter of which we may be reminded when we hear the complaint against the "Walhen" in Neidharts *'Ez gruonet wol die heide'* (below, Part III). KL 21 also includes words of summons addressed to individual nations--this time excluding Germany--as found in the pre-Hattin poem KL 7, *'Exsurgat gens Christiana.'* Albeit the echo is very weak: while all six stanzas of KL 7 are full of national designations with each of four stanzas devoted to a single people, KL 21 condenses the calls to four national groups in one four-line stanza (of thirteen stanzas total). Expectations of broad based European national support after Hattin were apparently difficult to uphold. Furthermore, in striking contrast to the pre-Hattin poem KL 6, *'Fides cum Ydolatria,'* in which we heard the crusader instructed to care for his family first, in KL 21 the crusader receives the opposite instructions to relinquish for the sake of the crusade love for children and relatives ("Cedat amor sanguinis et cognationum," 13,?).[45] Times have obviously changed in crusade recruiting, as indicated also by the special invitations to the very sinful ("qui sceleribus estis involuti," 7,1; cf., 6,2) to win indulgences by helping to remove the "(s)purci pompi germinis" (1,2) from their occupation of Jerusalem. There are surely solid reasons for the lack of unity and the floundering which Spreckelmeyer notes in KL 21,[46] one of which reasons may be desperation in the face of a daunting task. Hence, perhaps, the attempt to draw on poems from an earlier age during which being pro-crusade and propagandistic had come easier.

　　　In sum, to judge by the extant poems, the Battle of Hattin dealt a crushing blow to the Christian cause and triggered a dramatic change in their situation and outlook that is clearly reflected in Latin crusade poetry. The glib expectation and assurance of victory and the rejoicing over a success confidently expected to continue, gave way after Hattin to incomprehension and despair at defeat and to a desperate need to understand and explain the unexpected. God, who received very modest attention in the poetry composed while the Christian cause was going well, suddenly becomes the major focus of attention as the only sure resource of any hope for regaining lost Christian holdings (or else the focal point of bewilderment and incomprehension). And the savoring of very concrete and external details of Christian victory and of expansion both achieved and anticipated, is replaced after Hattin by an overriding tendency to look inward and to dwell on spiritual barriers, challenges,

and frontiers. It is an intriguing irony that the resounding victory of Saladin's army caused Latin crusade poets to appear more serious than their predecessors about Christianity, about its profound messages, about its God, and about the inner Christian self.

Who were these poets? Unfortunately, our information is meager indeed, and not only because most of the poems are transmitted anonymously. Even the six names that have been linked with individual poems are for the most part just names and not much more. The best known of these names is that of Marbod of Rennes who was a very gifted French poet of the early twelfth century and a bishop. As author of KL 4, '*In toto mundo*,' in praise of Bohemond of Taranto, Bishop Marbod is the only author known by name of a Latin crusade poem composed before the battle of Hattin.[47] KL 26, '*Homo cur properas*,' has been attributed by Anton Schmuck to Philip, Chancellor of the University of Paris in the early thirteenth century, but Schmuck's argumentation on the basis of content and style obviously does not convince Spreckelmeyer[48]; in his edition, Spreckelmeyer qualifies the name "Philip der Kanzler" as supposed author of KL 26 with a question mark.[49] Galfridus de Vino Salvo was the author of several works on rhetoric and literary style in one of which KL 24, '*Crux ego rapto*,' appears as an illustration of a literary point.[50] Richard of San Germano was a notary and the author of an important chronicle of southern Italy in which appears KL 25, '*Diro satis percussus vulnere*.'[51] About Berterus of Orléans and Erbo, to whom, respectively, are attributed KL 10, '*Juxta irenos Ieremie*,' and KL 15, '*Indue cilicium*,' we know essentially only the names listed in Roger of Hoveden's chronicle and the Vienna manuscript where, respectively, their poems appear.[52]

Otherwise, information about the poets is much less direct. KL 5, '*Nomen a solemnibus*,' is connected with the monastery of Solignac and was presumably composed by a monk.[53] The composer of KL 12, '*Plange, Sion et Iudaea*,' identifies himself as a refugee from Tarsus having found asylum in Sicily.[54] Spreckelmeyer makes the suggestion that the author of KL 16, '*Quod spiritu David precinuit*,' was himself a crusader who performed this poem in front of a crusading army.[55] It is unfortunate that Spreckelmeyer does not offer an explanation for this suggestion, for there is nothing obvious in the poem to support it. On the contrary, with its downplaying of the earthly war and its internalization of the crusade as spiritual matter of the crusader's soul-- to which Spreckelmeyer himself calls attention[56]--the poem might actually point away from crusade involvement.

In any case, the biographical indications available point unanimously to the clerical sphere as the milieu of all the Latin authors, and that probably means that they were not crusaders. Although we know that there were cases during the crusades where members of the clergy wielded the sword, definite references to this fact in Latin poetry of the crusade are inexistent: only in the pre-Hattin poem '*Ierusalem, civitas inclita*' (KL 9) did we hear a suggestion of clerics participating in warfare. With rare and isolated possible exceptions, they probably did not. In all likelihood, Latin crusade poetry is in the main the poetry of non-fighting, but otherwise acutely interested observers of crusade events and developments.

Introduction

A crusader for the purpose of this study is a person enlisted to bear arms in warfare against those whom European authorities, and especially the Church, declared to be the heathen enemies of Christianity, particularly the Christian Kingdom of Jerusalem, and of the Christian God. The poems treated in this section present a persona who is clearly identified as a crusader in this sense.

As noted previously, there are eight composers of German crusade poetry whose works fit this category: Friedrich von Hausen (c. 1150 - 1190), Hartmann von Aue (c. 1160 - early 13th century?), Albrecht von Johansdorf (c. 1165/1170 - early 13th century?), Reinmar der Alte (c. 1165 - early 13th century?), Otto von Botenlauben (documented 1196-1244), Hiltbolt von Schwangau (documented 1221-1256), Friedrich von Leiningen (died c. 1237), and Der Burggraf von Lienz (documented 1231-1258/69).

Of these eight poets, Friedrich von Hausen is probably the oldest, probably the first, and clearly a very important case in several respects. There are extant several poems by him featuring unambiguously a crusader as speaker. It has already been stated that Hausen's crusade participation is historically attested: Hausen died on the Third Crusade (1189-90) during a battle in present-day Turkey, that is, before actually reaching Palestine. His death occurred in May of 1190, roughly a month before the death of Emperor Frederick Barbarossa, the leader of this crusade, in whose administration Hausen was a high ranking official.[57] It should be noted, however, that precious little is reflected in Hausen's poems of his actual experience as a crusader. As with the rest of the poets in this group, some of whom he seems to have influenced considerably, Hausen's poems focus almost exclusively on the inner life of the crusader and say next to nothing about crusade activities and encounters.

Like Hausen, Otto von Botenlauben is also historically well attested: documents show him to have been born into a prominent family of the Franconian high nobility, and to have lived for considerably more than a decade in Palestine.[58] Unlike Hausen, Botenlauben is not historically attested as a crusader: he is assumed to have gone on the crusade of 1197, which began under the leadership of Barbarossa's son, Emperor Henry VI, but there are no documents extant which confirm that participation.

Of the six remaining poets in this group there is no historical record at all outside of literary texts.[59] Their poems are conceived, like those of Hausen and Botenlauben, from the viewpoint of the crusader. However, in the absence of historical documentation it cannot be determined whether the poets themselves were crusaders in every case. Opinions have varied on this point.

The poems of these eight poets share views of the crusades that are, in the main, quite different from those encountered in the Latin poems discussed above. In part it is a matter of emphasis: motifs that play an important role in the Latin poems play little or no role in the German. Certainly more interesting, however, are the differences between the two groups of poems in their treatment of themes and motifs common to both.

Our discussion of the German poems portraying crusaders will focus on four topics: 1) The Crusader and Jerusalem, 2) The Crusader and the Enemy, 3) The Crusader and God, and 4) The Crusader and Woman. The first three of these figure with varying prominence in both Latin and German crusade poetry. That the fourth, woman, is not prominent in Latin crusade poetry is probably not a surprise, but is also not insignificant. That absence can serve only to highlight the importance of woman in the lay crusade poems and provoke us to ponder the significance of this prominent female presence which, as we shall hear below, is probably not self-evident. The woman is portrayed in medieval German crusade poetry in a way that may suggest specific causes.

1. The Crusader and Jerusalem

Of all of the extant poetry composed by our eight poets, the city of Jerusalem is mentioned only in the poem *'Die hinnen varn'* (MF 89,21; KD 27)[60] by Albrecht von Johansdorf, which is transmitted in Manuscripts B and C .[61] The speaker in this poem has heard that there was never a greater need than now of help for Jerusalem, the pure city, as well as for the Holy Land:

> Die hinnen varn, die sagen dur got,
> daz Ierusalêm der reinen stat und ouch dem lande
> helfe noch nie noeter wart.
> (MF 89,21-23)

[Those who are leaving say for God's sake,
That Jerusalem and the whole country
Were never in greater need of help.]

Except for this passage, there is no mention in the poems portraying crusaders of any Palestinian place name associated either with the life of Jesus or with important events of the crusade. The crusader's attention remains fixed on the European homeland that he is about to leave or, in a few cases, has already left.

The fact that the quoted passage in Johansdorf's poem stands alone in this regard is an intriguing one. Jerusalem was, after all, the main goal of the crusade per se. That city was central and even crucial to the fulfillment of the crusade vow which, according to Brundage, was "a promise made to God to perform two acts: to journey to and visit the Holy Sepulchre in Jerusalem and to do so in the ranks of a general expedition to the Holy Land."[62] The quoted passage from Johansdorf's poem appears to echo this view.

By contrast, Latin crusade poetry is very explicit concerning both Jerusalem and other places important for crusade travel and warfare. In almost all of the extant Latin crusade poems there are references to at least a few places of importance. Six of the poems have the name Jerusalem (or Sion) in their first lines (KL 1, 2, 9, 12, 14, and 22). Dwelling at length on Jerusalem and other important places are, for example, the poems 'Ierusalem, laetare' (KL 2), 'Plange, Sion et Iudaea' (KL 12), and Erbo's 'Indue cilicium' (KL 15).

In German poems portraying the crusader, however, with the one said exception, the important locations of crusade events are apparently of no interest. As we shall hear continually, the eyes, hearts, and minds of the crusader in these poems are otherwise occupied.

2. The Crusader and the Enemy

The crusader portrayals of our eight poets also scarcely mention the enemy, and the few instances where they do so are all quite curious.

Friedrich von Hausen's well-known and much studied poem '*Mîn herze und mîn lîp diu wellent scheiden*' (MF 47,9; KD 24) is likewise transmitted in Manuscripts B and C, with differences that do not affect on our discussion. Here the crusader complains that his body wants to go and fight against the heathen ("der lîp wil gerne vehten an die heiden,' 47,11) while his heart wants to stay at home with his ladylove. Thus the enemy is mentioned here only incidentally in a passage whose main thrust is to reveal that the crusader is seriously torn between crusade obligation and amorous affection. An additional oddity is the fact that it is expressly the body, traditionally the source of carnality,[63] that "is said to be capable of what we should be allowed to call spiritual devotion,"[64] while it is the heart, traditionally the (more) spiritual side of the human makeup, that wants to stay with worldly love.[65]

The enemy is also mentioned only once in the extant poems of Albrecht von Johansdorf, and indeed in the above-mentioned poem in which the name of Jerusalem makes its only appearance in Middle High German crusade poetry (MF 89,21; KD 27). Here the speaker tries to provoke apparently hesitant potential recruits to go to Jerusalem's aid. He makes several fervent statements urging enlistment. Then, apparently fearing these to be insufficiently compelling, he accuses the heathen of insinuating that God's mother is not a virgin, an accusation for which, according to Hölzle, there is no historical verification.[66] However, even this provocative utterance seems insufficient to overcome all hesitation. In the last stanza of the poem we hear that our speaker (we assume that it is the same one) has been himself spending a lot of nights wondering how he can stay at home without losing God's favor ("waz sol ich wider got nu tuon, ob ich belîbe,/daz er mir genaedic sî?" 90,9f). He has even asked God to accept as a good thing ("vervâch ze guote," 90,15) his admittedly sinful love for a certain woman. Our speaker has thus apparently not been swayed by his own homiletic message.

The "heathen" are also mentioned once in the crusade poetry of Hartmann von Aue, namely in 'Ich var mit iuweren hulden' (MF 218,5; KD 38), transmitted only in Manuscript C. Here is named a specific group of "heathen," namely Saladin and his army ("Salatîn und al sîn her," (MF 218,19), that is, the victors in the Battle of Hattin mentioned above. This reference occurs in a passage involving a textual problem that may not be soluble. The two most important lines for the present purpose read as follows: "und lebte mîn her Salatîn und al sîn her, dienbraehten mich von Vranken niemer einen vuoz" (MF 218,19-20).

The insoluble textual problem is as follows. Depending upon how one analyzes and punctuates these lines (viz., comma after "her" or after "Salatîn"?), this passage can mean either (1) 'And if my lord were alive, Mr. Saladin and all his army would not (be able to) move me one foot out of Franconia,' or (2) 'And (even) if my lord Mr. Saladin and all his army were alive, they would not (be able to) move me one foot out of Franconia.'[67] In either case, Saladin and his army are not the focal point of a poem against the heathen, but are instead mentioned in passing during an emotional passage about the crusader's very reluctant separation from his homeland.

Interim Summary: The Crusader and the Enemy

In his poem '*In toto mundo*' (KL 4) in praise of Bohemond of Taranto, the bishop Marbod of Rennes mentions several groups who have been defeated by Bohemond or who, for fear of him, are ready to sue for peace. "Turcos," "Parthus, Arabs, Medus," and "Persus" are some of the proper names used to identify these groups. Similarly, in '*Heu, voce flebili*' (KL 11) and in '*Jerusalem, luge*' (KL 14), we encounter copious lists of names identifying the groups that make up the (in both cases victorious) enemy forces. In the poems of Latin poets, then, the enemy is identified quite specifically and in some detail.

By contrast, most of the German poems portraying crusaders-- that is: representatives of the lay warrior classes say nothing at all about that enemy. In the three poems by Hausen, Hartmann, and Johansdorf where the enemy is mentioned, his appearance is clearly overshadowed by more important concerns. In all three cases mentioned, those concerns have to do with attachment to the European homeland. Compared with Latin crusade poetry, this lack of interest in the heathen enemy is intriguing indeed. For it was, after all, members of the laity who were called upon to go and face the enemy in battle.

3. The Crusader and God

We recall that in the history of Latin crusade poetry, references to God underwent a striking change. In the poems composed before the Battle of Hattin, God is not mentioned at all in one poem (KL 8), and is overshadowed in several others (e.g., KL 1, 4, and 7) by earthly personalities and concerns. In the post-Hattin era, on the other hand, in a sudden surge of intense religiosity, almost every poem focuses on God--or Jesus--as the sin-punishing source of every reversal, or as the only hope either for victory over the Saracens or for inner renewal, and preferably both. We recall also that the post-Hattin group of Latin crusade poems is roughly coeval with the German tradition. Probably the first known German author of crusade poems, Friedrich von Hausen, participated in the crusade that was organized in explicit response to the Battle of Hattin and its aftermath.

Generally, the poets of the German tradition talk a lot less about God than their fellow-poets who composed in Latin. They also talk about God very differently. The intense focus on God, penitence, and the inner spiritual self in Latin poetry after Hattin has counterparts only rarely in the contemporary German poems. Here, as we shall hear, God is discussed in connection with very different matters.

Friedrich von Hausen

In the four extant crusade poems of Friedrich von Hausen there is strikingly little said about God or to God, and we shall hear at least one speaker in these poems who seems quite conscious of that fact. In addition, there is some tension in these poems between the view of the crusades as service to God and God's role within the poems. There are also indications that the crusader portrayed in the poems, and hence also the poet who created him, are quite aware of this tension.

'*Si darf mich des zîhen niht*'
(MF 45,37; KD 23)

According to the two manuscripts that transmit it, B and C, this poem consists of five stanzas of ten lines each. Each manuscript transmits the strophes in a different sequence, but Sayce sees all five as a unified whole.[68] According to the order in MS C followed by both editions used here (MF and KD), God is mentioned by name in the second and third stanzas, and is referred to a third time, in the fourth stanza, by a circumlocution ("dem der lônen kan" [to Him who knows how to reward], 46,38).

In the second stanza, the speaker invokes God to underscore his declaration of affection for his beloved:

ich bin ir holt: wenn ich vor gote getar,
sô gedenke ich ir.
(MF 46,13f)

[I love her. Whenever I dare before God
I think of her.][69]

Surely God can forgive him that, the speaker continues, for if it is a sin to think on her, then why did God make her so beautiful ("sô rehte wol getân," 46,18)?

In the third stanza, our speaker complains for seven lines about an infatuation that has kept him from pursuing wisdom ("wîsheit," 46, 23), noting in passing that many others complain about the same trouble (46,24f). He then announces his decision to devote himself to God ("an got gehaben," 46,26). He apparently feels the need to justify this decision: God can help people out of trouble, he explains; after all, no one knows how close one is to death (46,27f).

Apparently, whatever divine help is available, our speaker is having considerable difficulty turning to it and away from his unwise romance. He continues to reminisce about the history and woes of this attachment for nine lines of the fourth stanza. Only after an intense exercise in commemoration, does he repeat his decision, in the tenth and last line of the stanza, to serve God as someone who, unlike his lady love, knows how to reward ("der lônen kan," 46,38).

Even with this insight our speaker has still clearly not yet found divine relief. The fifth and last stanza of the poem finds him again mulling over the events of his long courtship in which, he insists, whatever harm ("schaden," 46,41) he suffered was undeserved. Then after devoting six more lines to fond remembrance of his worldly past, our crusader expresses (rather belated) regret that he has forgotten God for so long. The poem ends with another statement of the crusader's commitment to God, the formulation of which is just as unimpressive as the first two:

den wil ich iemer vor in allen haben
und in dâ nâch ein holdez herze tragen.
(MF 47,7f)

Hugo Bekker translates these lines as follows:

I shall hold him above them all forever,
and thereafter bear them a loving heart.[70]

The pronoun "them" can presumably refer only to women ("frowen") about whom the speaker insists in the sixth line of this final stanza that he would never say anything but good. Thus the quoted lines seem to say that God will have first place in his new life, but that women will be (and remain) second. God will presumably not receive another apology for the speaker's extended worldly reminiscing. One could actually suspect that our speaker has, in any case, only turned to God on the rebound from an unhappy romance. God has clearly not replaced this earthly attachment. On the contrary, the crusader states with pointed emphasis that God will be first but not alone in his devotion. Of course, one should perhaps recall that his inability to forget his old ways is ultimately God's fault. It was, after all, God who made the woman so attractive.

> *'Mîn herze und mîn lîp diu wellent scheiden'*
> (MF 47,9; KD 24)

This best known of Hausen's poems is transmitted in MSS B and C. Of the four transmitted strophes, B again presents a different order due to disturbance in transmission.[71]

God is mentioned three times in the poem, and here also in a manner that one can hardly characterize as fervent devotion. The first occurrence is in the last line of the first stanza. God is called upon to settle the conflict between the crusader's body, which wants to go fight the heathen, and his heart, which wants to stay at home with the lady love: "got eine müese scheiden noch den strît" (47,16) ["God alone must decide this disagreement"]. Thus the crusader declares himself neutral in the conflict. Seen another way, he reveals himself to be unable (or unwilling?) to devote himself entirely to the crusade by bringing his heart in line with the exigencies of the hour. Instead, the crusader proposes to devolve this responsibility onto God.

The second naming of God in this poem occurs in the stanza MF 47,25. It occurs in the context of a prayer which the crusader offers not on behalf of the body, which wants to go and do God's will, but on behalf of the heart, which does not. The crusader asks God to send this contrary heart to a place where it will be (well) received.[72] There is no basis in the passage for Bekker's tortuously argued proposal that the prayer "aims at God's compelling the heart away from love and towards the crusade."[73] On the contrary, with this prayer the crusader actually gives his blessings to the heart's rebellion against his own crusade obligations. Furthermore, the heart's rebellion ultimately flies in the face of the very God to whom the crusader is praying. Perhaps the incongruity can help explain why his prayer for the heart to be well received should be followed immediately by expressions of concern for its welfare:

> Owê! wie sol ez armen dir ergân?
> Wie getorstest du eine an solhe nôt ernenden?
> Wer sol dir dîne sorge helfen enden
>   mit triuwen, als ich hân getân?
> (MF 47,29-32)

> [Alas! How will it go with you poor thing?
> How do you dare brave such peril alone?
> Who will help you out of your care
> With devotion as I have done?]

Apparently, the good reception which the crusader prays for on the heart's behalf entails some kind of peril ("nôt") and worry ("sorgen") which the heart should not brave alone. And the crusader hints clearly that there is no help for the heart equal to his own. At this point it begins to become clear why the crusader offered no resistance to the heart's rebellion. Not only does the crusader sympathize with this rebellion, as indicated clearly by the formulation of his prayer; he also wants to benefit from it. The crusader is more than willing to provide accompaniment and protection to his heart in its desertion from crusade duty; in fact, there is no better man for the job.

Hausen's next use of God's name in this poem occurs at the beginning of the second stanza (MS C):

> Ich wânde ledic sîn von solicher swaere,
>   dô ich daz kriuze in gotes êre nam.
> (MF 47,17-18)

> [I thought myself free of such cares
> When I took the cross in the honor of God.]

Apparently, the crusader expected the taking of the cross to relieve him of any need to deal with uncooperative tendencies in his own personal makeup, such as a rebellious heart. Does this also mean that a clear (emotional/spiritual) commitment on his part was assumed to be God's responsibility, and not his? In any case, the crusader seems

to have assumed that with the taking of the cross the inner turmoil
which he is now experiencing, turmoil depicted in the personification
of a rebellious heart, would have been automatically done away. As in
'*Sî darf mich des zîhen niet*,' it is here again implied that God is to
blame for the problem. Just as there the crusader was bound to worldly
love because God made the woman so beautiful, here the crusader's
worldly heart problem persists because God's cross has not produced
the expected deliverance.

'*Min herze den gelouben hât*'
(MF 48,3; KD 25)

In this short poem of two stanzas transmitted in Manuscripts B
and C, God is mentioned twice. The first of these occurrences takes
place, once again, in a prayer. It is the prayer of a crusader, who has
already departed and is looking back longingly to his home on the
Rhine (48,3-6). He commits to God's care those whom he has left
behind for His sake:

herre got, ûf die genâde dîn
sô wil ich dir bevelhen die,
die ich durch dînen willen lie.
(MF 48,10-12)

[Lord God, to your grace
I want to commend those
Whom I have left for your sake.]

The second occurrence of God's name is found in the second
and last stanza of the poem. Here the departed crusader directs a
warning to the women who have stayed behind:

Ich gunde es guoten vrowen niet,
daz iemer mê koeme der tac
daz sî deheinen heten liep—
wan ez waere ir êren slac:
Wie kunde der gedienen iet?--
der gotes verte alsô erschrac.
(MF 48,13-18)

[I forbid good women
That the day should ever come

That they would love anyone
(For it would be a blow to their honor:
How could he be of any service?)
Who so feared God's expedition.]

In both these passages, the crusader looks back to his
homeland in concern. In the first, the concern expressed is for the loved
ones whom the crusader fears never to see again—as, we remember,
was indeed the case with the historical Hausen. In the second passage
the concern is for the spiritual welfare of the women left at home. The
crusader is worried that they may not be able to resist the advances of
opportunistic shirkers trying to reap advantage from the crusaders'
absences. God is called upon in the first passage to take care of the
loved ones whom the crusader has left behind for His sake ("durch
dînen willen," 48,12). In the second, service on "gotes verte" is invoked
as a test of courage and worthiness: men who are afraid to go are not
worthy of a good woman's love. In both cases, the God of the crusades
is invoked in support of an essentially worldly attachment to the
crusader's homeland.

> 'Si waenent dem tôde entrunnen sîn'
> (MF 53,31; KD 26)

In this poem of one stanza, transmitted in Manuscript C,
God's name occurs in the second of eight lines. The speaker warns
crusade shirkers who lie to God about the trip ("die gote erliegent sîne
vart") by taking the cross and then failing to go ("Swer daz kriuze nam
und niender vert," 53,35) that one day God will close in their faces the
door that He will open to His people.

As in the second stanza of Hausen's 'Mîn herze den gelouben
hat' discussed above, the speaker in 'Si waenet dem tôde entrunnen sîn'
also adopts a tone of homiletic moralizing to attack crusade shirkers.
Here the shirkers are those who had at first agreed to crusade duty and
had even taken the cross, but later reneged on their promise
("erliegent"). God is invoked as the judge who will exclude such
laggards when He opens the (heavenly) gate to His people (= faithful
crusaders). This is clearly an enhancement of the rather inconsequential
role of God that we have seen in Hausen's poetry so far. However,
comparison with Latin crusade poems, some of them contemporary
with the crusade poetry of Hausen, will show this enhancement to be
modest indeed.

The Latin poem describing the Hattin disaster, *'Heu, voce flebili'* (KL 11), was composed, Spreckelmeyer thinks, by a German countryman of Hausen within at most a decade of Hausen's own compositions.[74] In *'Heu, voce flebili,'* the speaker calls on "fratres and sorores" to pour out penitent hearts in prayer to God, the "gloria iustorum, angelorum bonitas, and salus peccatorum," who once became angry with His own people Israel because of their sin.[75] In the Latin poem *'Tonat evangelica clara vox in mundo'* (KL 23), which, according to Spreckelmeyer, was presumably composed by a German cleric,[76] young men in particular are called upon to let the cross draw their hearts and minds to things in the hereafter ("cape mente, cogita corde de futuris") since the ax is now laid at the root of the tree (Matthew 3:10).[77] In the Latin poem *'Christiani nominis'* (KL 21), presumably composed, according to Spreckelmeyer,[78] on the Third Crusade that cost Hausen his life, the crusader is called upon to dispense with love of children and relatives ("Cedat amor sanguinis et cognationum") for the sake of God and crusade.[79] In comparison with these poems, Hausen's *'Ich gunde es guoten vrowen niet'* (MF 48,13; KD 25-II) appears in a different light. Its focus and the root of its passionate outburst are the same as in Hausen's *'Mîn herze den gelouben hât,'* that is, concern and fascination with the figure of the crusade shirker who can enjoy the comforts of home while the crusader braves the rigors and dangers of crusade duty. The crusade shirker is a troubling and vexing stock figure of the vernacular poetry of the laity. We shall encounter him again in Heinrich von Rugge's *Leich* (MF 98,28 - 99,2; KD 32), in Reinmar's *'Durch daz ich vröide hie bevor ie gerne pflac'* (MF 181,5-12; KD 40), and probably in the Occitan poet Marcabru's *'A la Fontana del vergier'* (KD 11).

Thus also in *'Si waenent dem tôde entrunnen sîn,'* as indeed in all of Hausen's crusade songs, God's role is important only in connection with essentially worldly concerns and specifically with those related to the crusader's homeland. In their conception of God and in the attitude expressed in them toward God, Hausen's crusade songs and the Latin crusade poetry of his day are worlds apart.

Hartmann von Aue

Of the three extant crusade poems of Hartmann von Aue, God is
mentioned explicitly only in '*Dem kriuze zimet wol reiner muot*' (MF
209,25; KD 36). There is an indirect reference to God in '*Swelch vrowe
sendet lieben man*' (MF 211,20; KD 37), the poem of one stanza where
the woman is called upon to pray for her beloved man on crusade.
There is no mention of God in the three long strophes of '*Ich var mit
iuweren hulden*' (MF 218,5; KD 38) where the speaker is going on
crusade at the command of love ("diu minne," 218,9f).

> '*Dem kriuze zimet wol reiner muot*'
> (MF 209,25; KD 36)

It is in intriguing contrast to the other two crusade poems of
Hartmann that God is named all of seven times in the six strophes of
'*Dem kriuze zimet wol reiner muot*' (MF 209,25), of which strophes 1-
4 are transmitted in MS. B and all six in MS. C.[80] The first occurrence
falls in the seventh line of the second stanza. After having spent the
first stanza reporting the wishes of the personified cross, the speaker
reinforces its challenging message in his own words:

> swes schilt ie was zer welte bereit
> ûf hôhen prîs,
> ob er den gote nû verseit,
> der ist niht wîs.
> (MF 210,3-6)

> [Whoever has up to now devoted his shield
> To the world for its praise,
> If he now denies it to God,
> He is not wise.]

These words are addressed specifically to knights, "ritter" (209,37). The
name of God thus first occurs in a statement which pointedly invokes the
knightly world. The speaker goes on to promise that whoever has good
fortune there ("dâ wol gevert," 210,8), presumably meaning on the field of
crusade warfare, will receive both the praise of the world and the salvation
of the soul ("der welte lop, der sêle heil," 210,10).

God is mentioned in this poem for the second time--this time
in the person of Christ--in the ninth line of the third strophe. This

occurrence of God's name is again preceded by a personification, but not of the cross as in the first instance. Here it is the world's turn to be personified. The world is pictured as a smiling woman who beckons to the speaker enticingly (210,11f). He berates himself for having been silly enough to follow her, running after her for many a day ("manigen tac," 210,15) and hurrying under her sway to places where no one can find anything that lasts ("dâ niemen staete vinden mac," 210,17). In this pressure situation, the speaker cries out for divine aid:

> Nu hilf mir, herre Krist,
> der mîn dâ vârende ist,
> daz ich mich dem entsage
> mit dînem zeichen, daz ich hie trage.
> (MF 210,19-22)

> [Now help me, Lord Christ,
> Against the one who stalks me,
> That I may resist him
> With the sign that I am wearing.]

It is interesting that the personification of the world as seductive woman is not retained in the prayer. Here the being whose enticement the speaker wishes to resist is designated as a male. In Walther von der Vogelweide's 'Frô Welt, ir sult dem wirte sagen' (L 100,24), of which Hartmann's poem is a strikingly similar predecessor, there is likewise an intriguing alternation between the beguiling Dame World and the masculine "wirt" (100,24) lurking in the background. It is noteworthy that while at the end of Walther's 'Frô Welt," Walther (she addresses him by name) states that no one can protect himself ("bewarn") from the snare ("lâge," 101,19) of Dame World, this protection is precisely what the speaker in Hartmann's poem expects from the "zeichen," the cross, that he is wearing. With this reference to his apparel, by the way, the speaker identifies himself clearly as a crusader. And, as in Hausen's 'Mîn herze und mîn lîp diu wellent scheiden' (MF 47,9; KD 24), it is here again suggested that the cross is expected to free the crusader from the snares of worldly care.

The third occurrence of God's name in Hartmann's 'Dem kriuze zimet wol reiner muot' falls in the twelfth and last line of stanza four. In the previous eleven lines of this stanza our crusader has been lamenting and eulogizing his deceased lord, whose death seems to have been a severe personal loss. Now that the lord is dead, it no longer interests our crusader how the world stands ("swie nû diu werlt nâch im gestât," MF 210,12). In death the lord took with him the best part of the crusader's joy ("der vröide mîn den besten teil," 210,27); it would (therefore?) be the sensible thing for him to attain the salvation of his soul: "schüefe ich nû der sêle heil,/ daz waer ein sin" (210,29f). If it should be possible for his lord to share--posthumously, as it were--in the benefits of his crusade service, the crusader is willing to share with him half the benefits ("im ir halber jehen," 210,33). It is noteworthy that this offer to share his crusader benefits with his departed lord does not seem to have been supported by contemporary church law.[81] In any case, it is in this context that the name of God falls in the almost casually expressed hope to see the deceased lord again before God's throne ("vor gote," 210,34). Once again the role of God is that of a bystander witnessing an important event. That the crusader and his lord will share the reward for the former's crusade service is simply presumed. It is apparently self-evident that God will, of course, look on in approval while this takes place.

God is next mentioned in the fifth stanza and for the second time in Hartmann's poem by the name of Christ. The crusader tells us that his joy ("vröide") was never free of care ("sorgelôs,") until the days ("tage") came when he caught sight of Christ's flowers ("Kristes bluomen," 210,35-37), the insignia on the crusader's clothing. This insignia announces a summer time ("kündet eine sumerzît") as a beautiful prospect ("in süezer ougenweide") for the crusader's future (210,39-211,2). The crusader continues with a prayer for God's help:

> got helfe uns dar
> Hin in den zehenden kôr,
> dar ûz ein hellemôr
> sîn valsch verstôzen hât
> und noch den guoten offen stât.
> (MF 211,3-7)

> [May God help us on
> To the tenth choir,
> From which a moor of hell
> Was ejected by his misdeed,
> But which still stands open to the good.]

In Hausen's '*Mîn herze und mîn lîp diu wellent scheiden*,' we heard the crusader complain that the donning of the cross has **failed** to free him from worldly cares. In Hartmann's '*Dem kriuze zimet wol reiner muot*,' on the other hand, putting on "Kristes bluomen" seems to have had the desired effect: the crusader here is indeed free of care. Or, at least, so he claims.

The fact is, however, that the powerful and dangerous attraction of the world continues to be in evidence in the lines that follow. The final stanza, in which also the final occurrence of "got" takes place, begins with one last look at the world. In stanza three, the world appeared as an alluring woman. Stanza six reintroduces the world without explicit personification, but in terms that definitely call it to mind:

> Mich hat diu welt also gewent
> daz mir der muot
> sich zeiner maze nâch ir sent
> --dêst mir nu guot,
> got hât vil wol ze mir getân,
> als ez nu stat,
> daz ich der sorgen bin erlân--,
> diu menigen hât
> Gebunden an den vuoz,
> daz er belîben muoz,
> swanne ich in Kristes schar
> mit vröiden wunneclîche var.
> (MF 211, 8-19)

> [The world has brought me to the point
> That I long (only)
> Modestly for it
> (That is good,
> God has been good to me,
> As it turns out,
> That I am freed from its cares)
> Which still holds many
> Bound by the foot
> So that he must remain behind
> While I go in Christ's entourage
> With manifold joys.]

In this stanza the crusader claims that he has escaped from the world and joined the fold of Christ. However, the formulation of the stanza makes the escape appear rather curious. First, the crusader credits the world with having caused ("gewent") his desire for the world itself to diminish. MHG *wenen* (modern German *gewöhnen*) means 'to make one accustomed to.' Thus, strictly speaking, the world is presented as being in charge. God is praised for having been good to the crusader, but is never expressly credited with an active role: The freeing of the crusader from worldly cares is expressed passively: "daz ich der sorgen bin erlân." In the formulation of the stanza as transmitted, only the world has been explicitly credited with bringing the crusader to this point of freedom. And the active role of the alluring world is further underscored when the crusader contrasts his new liberated state to the situation of those whom the world still holds bound by the foot. Precisely what was the nature of this "liberation"?

In Friedrich von Hausen's '*Sî darf mich des zîhen niet*' we heard a crusader turn to a God who knows how to reward (MF 46,29-38) because his service to his lady has gone unrewarded. Thus God received the crusader's service on the rebound from a bad experience in worldly love. Here in Hartmann's '*Dem kriuze zimet wol reiner muot,*' God is made to appear unimpressive as the recipient into His fold of a knight who, under unclear circumstances, has been liberated by the world from the latter's own grasp. Has this knight perchance also joined up with God after experiencing failure in the world?

The unimpressiveness of God's appearance in Hartmann's poem can be pointed up clearly by comparison with Latin poetry. First of all, in Latin poetry God is mentioned much more often; in comparison with with the six occurrences in the seventy-two lines of Hartmann's '*Dem kriuze zimt wol reiner muot,*' for example, there are in the forty-eight lines of '*Tonat evangelica*' (KL 23) thirteen express namings of God, usually in the name form Christ. Perhaps more important is the difference between the two poems in the manner in which God is presented. '*Tonat evangelica*' refers to God explicitly, vividly and usually as an actor: the first stanza promises that God will illuminate and save the soul from all ills; in stanza two, the cross of Christ admonishes the young man to consider his creator (cf. Ecclesiates 12:1) and to think upon the future day when the ax will be laid at the root of the tree (cf. Matthew 3:10); in stanza three, old men are called to true penitence through the cross of Christ ("vera penitentia cruce Christi"); stanza four announces the coming reign of God; and on it goes in this vein for twelve very biblical stanzas.

By comparison, as already indicated, the presence of God in Hartmann's poem is strikingly understated: the crusader tells the knights in stanza two that whoever has always had a ready shield when it came to the high praise of the world ("zer welte bereit/ ûf hôhen prîs," 210,3f) is not wise to now deny (the service of that shield to) God. For, as he adds later, it is great to have both the praise of the world and the salvation of the soul (210,9f). We noted earlier that, during the course of the poem, the crusader seems to abandon this proposed striving for the favor of both God and world, and even to decry his earlier attempt to please both. Still, we noted that what he says about God after this change in attitude remains quite unimpressive, and comparison with 'Tonat evangelica' can only underscore this fact. Specifically, the crusader prays to God to help him use His "zeichen," the cross (210,22), to resist his old ways which are therewith revealed to be a continuing danger for him ("vârende," 210,20). He next mentions God, almost casually, in expressing his willingness to share his reward for crusading with his deceased lord and his desire to see him again before God ("vor gote," 210,34) whose favor on this intent seems to be assumed. Otherwise, the crusader mentions Christ once to point out that he is wearing "Kristes bluomen" (210,37), prays to God for a boost into the tenth heavenly choir (211,3f), and (smugly?) contrasts his own future "in Kristes schar" (211,19) with the fate of those whom he will leave behind "gebunden an den vuoz" (211,16). In sum, while in 'Tonat evangelica' God is the powerful focal point of worship and awe, in Hartmann's 'Dem kriuze zimet wol reiner muot' God is invoked in a way that makes Him appear ancillary, rather passive, and comparatively insignificant in connection with a number of issues which seem more important.

The Latin poem 'Tonat evangelica clara vox in mundo' (KL 23) was composed, according to Spreckelmeyer, sometime in the second half of the 12th century after the battle of Hattin, and presumably by a German cleric.[82] If one dates Hartmann's 'Dem kriuze zimet wol reiner muot' in connection with the Third Crusade, then it was probably composed at about the same time as 'Tonat evangelica'; or if with the crusade lead initially by Emperor Henry VI, then less than a decade later.[83] Both the Latin and the German poem feature the cross prominently in their message of challenge. In its second stanza, 'Tonat evangelica' issues a special call to young men, charging them to remember the cross and let it be a constant admonishment, considering future things in their minds and hearts: "cape mente, cogita corde de futuris" (2,3). One thinks immediately about the cross's requirement of "reiner muot and kiusche site" in Hartmann's opening sentence (MF 209,25f). But the Latin poem also has a message from the cross for the old and decrepit ("Senes et decripiti"), namely a call to penitence by the cross of Christ ("vera penitentia cruce Christi"). Neither this age group nor a message of penitence figures in Hartmann's *'Dem kriuze zimet wol reiner muot.'* The omission of penitence in the German poem is by no means self-evident when one considers that Hartmann is also the author of a story entitled *Gregorious* in which (1) the titular hero's father dies on a penitential pilgrimage to the Holy Grave and (2) the hero himself later spends seventeen years doing penitence on a rock in the sea.[84]

In stanza seven of *'Tonat evangelica,'* an emotional appeal is issued to the soul to rise from the depths and flee earthly and (hence) impure things (7,1-2). In order to avoid shipwreck, this soul is advised to navigate by the cross of Christ (7,3-4). Hartmann's crusader uses similar terms when he warns his fellow knights (MF 209,37) about the beguiling world that has exercised great sway on him up to now. In the Latin poem, the soul is characterized as sinful soul ("peccatrix anima" KL 23,5,1) in need of cleansing from "omni crimine" (5,2) and called upon to glory in the cross of Christ in order to be liberated from the enemy, here undoubtedly meaning the devil.[85] This kind of language finds no place in Hartmann's poem which is addressed not to potential penitents, but to men of the knightly class, men of attainment ("erwerben," 209,28), of control and skill ("meisterschaft," 209,31), men accustomed to paying their dues through effort ("zinsent," 209,37). Hartmann talks about God in a poem addressed to knights as men of substance and stature.

> *"Swelch vrowe sendet ir lieben man'*
> (MF 211,20; KD 37)

This poem, transmitted in Manuscripts B and C, is only seven lines long. Its words are addressed to women and enjoin them to send their dear men on the crusade in the right frame of mind ("mit rehtem muote," 211,21). The woman is also called upon to pray for the beloved crusader while he is away. However, despite these religious elements, the poem is actually quite worldly. In fact, it complements the *Frauenstrophe* in *'Mîn herze den gelouben hât'* (MF 48,3; KD 25) by Friedrich von Hausen discussed above. In the latter, women are warned not to risk disgrace ("laster," 48,22) by taking up with a man who is afraid ("erschrac," 48,18) to go on crusade. Hartmann's poem is a more positively formulated exhortation to women, but contains essentially the same pointed warning. Here the woman is promised a share in her crusader's reward ("halben lôn," 211,22) on the condition that she maintain herself at home in such a way that she merits a good reputation ("kiusche wort," 211,24). In neither of the two poems does God figure prominently in regard to a concern that is basically a worldly one. Both sermonize in connection with a matter between knightly crusaders and the ladies from whom in their absence they expect and demand supportive and impeccable behavior, thus a matter to be addressed on the horizontal plane of earthly interaction.

> *'Ich var mit iuweren hulden'*
> (MF 218,5; KD 38)

In this poem of twenty-four lines, transmitted only in Manuscript C, there is likewise no explicit reference to God. There is also no mention of the cross. Nor does the speaker indicate anything specific about (the purpose of) his travel. From his reference to Saladin together with the revelation that his travels are taking him over seas ("über mer," 218,18) we can surely assume that he is going on crusade, but he never actually tells us so. In fact, he seems at pains to be cryptic, with the result that one has to form judgments based solely on circumstantial evidence.

For instance, the crusader tells us that he is going because love, "minne," captured him, extracted a pledge of security ("sicherheit") from him, and has now commanded him to go ("daz ich var," 218,9f). Later in the poem, love, "minne," is again credited with taking him away from his home (literally: his native tongue) over seas: "nu seht, wie sî mich ûz mîner zungen ziuhet über mer" (218,18). Scholars have continually noted that the manner in which the crusader speaks about *minne* in this poem gives the initial impression of a worldly love. Still, while duly noting this worldly appearance, scholars have continued to insist that this "minne" which the crusader credits with (or blames for?) causing him to be a crusader must necessarily be love of God, *gottesminne*[86]. However that may be, the fact is that Hartmann leaves God unmentioned and presents love in a noticeably worldly guise.

Blattmann points out that the description of *minne*'s capturing the crusader and exacting a pledge of security from him is based on the language of the tournament.[87] Thus, here also, Hartmann's terminology indicates an emphatically knightly conception of crusading. Just as the call to participation in '*Dem kriuze zimet wol reiner muot*' (MF 209,25) was issued specifically to knights (209,37), so also here the speaker has been metaphorically drafted by capture and sent on crusade from the midst of knightly activity. Furthermore, it is not clear that he has gone willingly, and indeed the language of the poem indicates that it has not necessarily been his choice to do so, and certainly not an enthusiastic one. And on this critical point Hartmann again echoes Friedrich von Hausen.[88] Just as the crusader in Hausen's '*Mîn herze den gelouben hât*' (MF 48,3) maintains that it is only because of love ("durch liebe oder durch der minne rât," 48,5) that he is not still on the Rhine ("noch alumbe den Rîn," 48,6), so here in Hartmann's '*Ich var mit iuweren hulden,*' the crusader insists quite similarly that it is *minne* that drew him "ûz mîner zungen...über mer" (218,18). And if it were not for his loyalty and oath ("mîne triuwe und mînen eit,"218,12) to *minne*, which he has no intention of breaking ("wic kûme,"), Saladin and all his army could not move him one foot out of his homeland ("Salatîn und al sîn her/ dien braehten mich von Vranken niemer einen vuoz," 218,20).

Whatever remains to be said about the ultimate implications of this much disputed passage, one thing is certain: it is not clear that God figures very prominently in it and it seems fairly certain that He does not. The crusader's entlistment results from his defeat at the hands of *minne*. It is widely assumed that *gottesminne* is to be understood, but it is nowhere stated or made clear. What is clear is that this (unwilling?) crusade enlistee is a worthy opponent of *minne* with fine knightly qualities.[89] That he is a man of resolve is expressed in his stalwart declaration that his going is a foregone conclusion: "ez ist unwendic, ich muoz endelîchen dar" (218,11). His word is his bond: breach of his oath would be inconceivable (218,12). One also hears in his words a very palpable sense of his superiority to unnamed others, a sense of superiority that we also detected in '*Dem kriuze zimet wol reiner muot*' (MF 209,25; KD 36). In both poems, the speaker is at pains to make clear that crusading is not for the fainthearted and wishy-washy, but for knights of bodily temperance ("sînem lîbe meisterschaft," (209,31) and loyalty ("triuwe," 218,12). In both poems, the crusader also explicitly contrasts himself with others: in MF 209,25 he rejoices about having escaped the cares which have bound many by the foot, keeping them back while he travels in "Kristes schar" (211,15-19); in MF 218,5 he lords it over the "minnesinger"--or fellow-*minnesinger*, since he himself "mac wol von minnen singen" (218,23)--who suffer from wasteful vain imaginings, "wân" (218,22 and 26), foolishly missing out on the superior *minne* that he now knows and possesses (218,24f and 28).

In sum, while one has to conjecture how much or how little God has had to do with his decision, the crusader in Hartmann's poems has made certain to present himself as a dedicated and superior knight who can be counted on to keep the *sicherheit* that he has sworn to love, whether earthly or divine.

Albrecht von Johansdorf

In the poetry of Johansdorf, God is a much more substantial presence than in the poetry of Hartmann. While God's name appears seven times in Hartmann's crusade poetry, all of those in one of the three crusade poems under his name, God's name appears in all five of Johansdorf's crusade poems a total of eighteen times. Furthermore, the manner in which God appears or is addressed in Johansdorf's crusade poetry is much more clearly suitable to the divine role in the crusades than was the case in Hartmann's works.

To be sure, in Johansdorf's poetry the name of God occurs a few times as an incidental name and not clearly as an important presence. Excluding MF 88,10, which is based on editorial conjecture, there are three of these instances where the name of God occurs without real significance in the formulation of an oath or an oath-like expression. One is found in the poem '*Mich mac der tôt von ir minnen wol scheiden*' (MF 87,5; KD 38), transmitted in Manuscript A, where the crusader supports his claim of innocence by declaring himself cursed before God as a heathen ("vervluochet vor gote alse ein heiden," 87,10) if he has done anything to deserve the anger of his beloved. Similarly, in '*Ich und ein wîp*' (MF 87,29—both versions[90]; KD 30) a crusader whose beloved apparently fears that his departure means that he is leaving her for good, swears to her that God should not save him from hell ("got vor der helle niemer mich bewar," MF 87,35) if he hedges any such intention. Finally, there is the report in the opening line of '*Die hinnen varn*' (MF 89,21; KD 27), transmitted in B and C, that those about to depart are saying "durch got" ("by God"?) that Jerusalem was never in greater need of help. This invoking of God likewise seems to be a turn of phrase in which the naming of God has no real substantial importance.

In several instances, however, and in striking contrast to Hartmann, Johansdorf's poetry refers to God in ways that clearly show

Him recognition and respect as crusade divinity. A number of these references are formulated in terms that are readily associated with traditional orthodox crusade language.[91] When in *'Mich mac der tôt'* (MF 87,5; KD 28), for instance, the crusader tells his distressed "herzevrowe" that crusaders have to go in the honor of the mighty God ("dur des rîchen gotes êre," 87,23), here we are surely hearing a reference to God that goes beyond the merely formulaic. The same holds for the crusader's explanation in *'Ich und ein wîp'* (MF 87,29; KD 30) that (Christian) losses in battle result from God's anger ("dâ bî sô merkent gotes zorn," 88,28a/"an den man siht den gotes zorn," 88,28b); such an explanation is also invoked several times in Latin crusade poetry after Hattin to explain Christian defeats.[92] In *'Die hinnen varn'* (MF 89,21: KD 27), we hear a crusader bemoan the faith and fate of those who are able to go to God's aid and fail to do so ("der gote wol hulfe und tuot es niht" 89,34), and in *'Guote liute, holt die gâhe'* (94,15), good people are exhorted to go and fetch the gift that the Lord gives to crusaders. In both cases, God is named in reference to serious matters of crusade commitment: in the latter poem, potential crusaders are reminded that God has given them body and soul ("got hat iu beide sêle und lîp gegeben" 94,23), a message to the sluggish about indebtedness and obligation to God that reminds one of the Latin crusade poem *'Crux ego rupta queror'* (KL 24).

Given such serious expressions of crusade commitment, one finds all the more striking those references to God in Johansdorf's poems that betray a quite different outlook. For instance, the crusader in *'Ich und ein wîp'* (87,29) attempts to assuage the fears of a beloved woman who opposes his crusade involvement by proclaiming the following "theological dictum"[93]:

> Swer minne minneclîche treit
> gar âne valschen muot,
> des sünde wirt vor gote niht geseit.
> Si tiuret und ist guot.
> (MF 88,33-35)

> [Whoever loves lovingly,
> Entirely without false intent,
> His sin will not be declared before God;
> It elevates and is good.]

Sincere love, then, will help the lover with his sin problem. Love is here "unabashedly and openly associated with Christian morality" and "makes the *ritter* more amenable to Christian morality and more worthy of God's favor."[94] As such, this love also enters into competition with the crusade itself, which is expressly purported to provide the crusader with forgiveness of sins. Here, however, absolution is declared not by a pope or any other church official, but rather by a crusader in love.

The question of how God views the love of man for woman comes up in a slightly different but no less startling way in *'Die hinnen varn'* (MF 89,21). After two stanzas of passionate and provocative sermonizing, a "dedicated crusader and crusade evangelist"[95] is heard to admit that he has been asking himself for many a night what he will do to attain God's grace if he stays behind:

> ich gedenke alsô vil manige naht,
> 'waz sol ich wider got nu tuon, ob ich belîbe,
> daz er mir genaedic sî?'
> (MF 90,8-10)

> [I spend many a night thinking,
> What shall I do for God, if I stay behind,
> So that he will be merciful to me?]

At this delicate moment, the crusader takes stock of his sins apparently to determine if he has one or more to spare. His quick inventory reveals that he does not have any really big sins except for one that he is not prepared to relinquish. He sums up his situation as follows:

> Sô weiz ich niht vil grôze schulde, die ich habe,
> niuwan eine der kume ich niemer abe.
> alle sünde liez ich wol wan die:
> ich minne ein wîp vor al der welte in mînem muote.
> got herre, daz vervâch ze guote!
> (MF 90,11-15)

> [Actually, I do not know of any great sin that I have
> Except for one which I will never relinquish.
> All sin I will leave off except for one:
> I love a woman more than all the world in my heart.
> Lord God, accept that for good.]

And with this pointed announcement, the poem ends. We heard a similar ending previously in *'Sî darf mich des zîhen niht'* by Friedrich von Hausen. There a crusader, regretting that he has forgotten God so long (MF 47,5f), declares that he will now place Him first, but will also continue to have a devoted heart for women as (close?) second priority. The *minne*-smitten crusader in Johansdorf's *'Die hinnen varn'* indicates no such order of priorities, and his final words to God are also **not** formulated so as to make clear that God will be put first. Actually, God is presented with a *fait accompli* and asked--or told--to accept for good(ness?) the circumstance that the crusader loves a woman in his heart above all the world.

One final passage merits attention in a similar vein, namely in *'Guote liute, holt die gâbe'* (MF 94,15; KD 29) whose complex transmission need not concern us.[96] In this passage, Johansdorf again portrays a sermonizing speaker. After exhorting good people to go and fetch the boon which God has waiting for them and to earn His reward with joys ever manifold ("mit vröiden iemer manecvalt," 95,20), our crusader is suddenly heard begging *minne* to let him go free. This freedom, as he is careful to let *minne* know, is to be only temporary. As soon as he has finished this pure journey of God ("die reinen gotes vart," (94,29), *minne* will be welcome again. He thus hopes that the crusades will be merely an interruption in his hearty relationship with *minne*. The lack of devotion to God implied in this statement becomes increasingly clear in the words which the crusader next addresses to *minne*:

> Wilt aber dû ûz mînem herzen scheiden niht
> --daz vil lîhte unwendic doch beschiht--,
> vüere ich dich danne mit mir in gotes lant.
> sô sî er der guoten dort um halben lôn gemant.
> (MF 94,34)

> [However, if you do not want to exit my heart
> --which can, of course, easily happen—
> Then I will take you with me into God's land,
> So let him be reminded of the half-reward for the good woman.]

Thus the crusader essentially cancels the interruption in his *minne*-relationship. "What is perhaps no more that a half-hearted *Minneabsage* thus becomes *Minnebehauptung*."[97] He will not demand that worldly love leave his heart even for the duration of the Holy

Cause. If *minne* does not want to leave the crusader's heart, he will simply take *minne* along to "gotes lant." God will apparently have to put up with a stowaway in the crusader's entourage.

With this decision, the crusader spares himself the conflict between service to God and attachment to worldly love suffered by the crusader in the poems of Hausen and, as we shall hear a little later, also in the poems of Reinmar. Nevertheless, as he adds immediately, he still expects God to give the half-reward to which he considers his lady-love to be entitled: "sô sî er der guoten dort umb halben lôn gemant."

For Bekker's attempt to explain this passage by suggesting that "the persona may be saying that with his request granted, the lady may look upon herself as another soldier in God's legions,"[98] there is simply no basis in the text. For one thing, the crusader does not make a request. In fact, he apparently finds no need to address God directly, but rather admonishes Him indirectly in words addressed to *minne*. Sudermann also credits the crusader with a "self-revelatory prayer"[99] which does not take place. Apparently, it is God's role to fulfill the indirectly expressed expectations of a crusader who, like his counterpart in Hausen's '*Sî darf mich des zîhen niet*' (MF 45,37), has expressly declined to break with worldly love.

Clearly, then, while the role of God in the poetry of Albrecht von Johansdorf is a substantial one, He is not addressed and talked about as a deity inspiring awe, fear, or even great respect. On the contrary, as in the crusade poetry of Hausen, by implication God is called upon to adjust to the inclinations of a crusader for whom apparently the place of supremacy is occupied not by God, but rather by *minne*, earthly love for earthly woman.

Reinmar der Alte

In the two poems by Reinmar der Alte that portray a crusader, the word *got* appears six times. To these must be added a reference to the Virgin Mary, who is also mentioned in a crusade poem of Johansdorf. There, however, she is not invoked as a deity; rather the crusader in Johansdorf's *'Die hinnen varn'* (MF 89,21), in an attempt to provoke lethargic potential crusaders to enthusiastic enlistment, reports an alleged saying of the heathen that the mother of God is not a virgin ("daz gotes muoter niht sî ein maget," MF 90,2). In the second of the two poems by Reinmar discussed below (MF 181,13), however, Mary is a deity to whom the crusader addresses a prayer for divine aid.

Both of the crusade poems of Reinmar are published only in Manuscript C. In the first and, if one can judge by the contents, apparently the earlier of the two poems (MF 180,28), God is mentioned four times. Since the fourth is a mild oath in support of the speaker's opinion ("weiz got," 181,12), only the first three occurrences merit discussion in this context.

In Reinmar's *'Durch daz ich vröide hie bevor ie gerne pflac'* (MF 180,28; KD 40), the crusader refers to the crusade to explain his sad behavior, which is apparently not characteristic of him. To be sure, he is now just as capable of joy ("vröide," MF 180,28) as he ever was, but has relinquished it out of respect for God ("des geswîgte ich durch die gotes êre," 180,33). However, he quickly points out that come the living day ("ein lebender tac," 180,31) when the crusade is over, he will be able to do everything that he ever could and more ("daz ich ie kunde oder mêre," 180,32). Thus, as in *'Guote liute, holt die gâbe'* (MF 94,15) by Johansdorf, the crusade is pictured as an interruption in a life of worldly pleasure. Unlike Johansdorf, however, Reinmar does not have the crusader explicitly favor continuing this joyous life uninterruptedly by taking *vröide* with him to "gotes lant." On the contrary, he claims to have undergone a genuine change in his life: since God has given him so many blessings ("saelden," 180,34), he announces, he would be a fool ("gouch") if he did not acknowledge them ("erkennen").

This adherence to appropriate crusading behavior intensifies in the second stanza of the poem. In painting a strikingly favorable picture of the crusade, Reinmar seems to echo the northern French crusader Conon de Béthune.[100] In the second stanza of Conon's influential poem *'Ahi, Amors, com dure departie'* (KD 20) the crusader there calls on great and small to go practice chivalry ("faire chevallerie") where one can gain paradise, honor, respect, laud and praise, as well as the love of his beloved ("paradis et honor/ et pris et los, et l'amor de s'amie"). Reinmar reproduces a slightly abbreviated selection of these gains, namely: praise and honor and in addition God's favor ("lop und êre und doch dar zuo gotes hulde," 181,1). Intriguingly, Reinmar has the crusader delay mention of the love of woman until the third and last stanza of the poem, which will concern us later. In view of these gains, the crusader goes on, there is really no reason ("âne schulde," 180,37) for anyone to be sad. He even prays to God ("got helfe im," 181,2) for the poor soul who can be downcast in spite of such obvious benefits. However, he is also strikingly attentive to the sad thoughts of this pitiable creature who holds joy in low esteem ("vröide...harte unwert," 180,36) and who, instead of rejoicing, endures with sorrow ("mit sorgen dulde," 181,2), and thereby detracts from the value of his service ("ein dienest niemer guot.../ den man sô rehte trûreclîche tuot," 181,3f).

Furthermore, while the crusader himself projects this sad behavior on an anonymous foil ("manigem man," 180,36), we cannot help but remember that the poem began with his reporting that it is his own uncharacteristic sad behavior that has attracted public attention. It thus appears that, as in Johansdorf's 'Die hinnen varn' (MF 89,21) and 'Guote liute, holt die gâbe' (MF 94,15), here also the crusader's message for others stands at odds with his own inner outlook. Despite his efforts to respond appropriately to the goodness of God and to this occasion for joy called the crusade, he cannot escape the fact that his own demeanor and frame of mind is basically sad.

In "Des tages dô ich daz kriuze nam' (MF 181,13; KD 39), God is mentioned twice, to which, as indicated above, we must add the Virgin Mary since the crusader utters a prayer for help to her as a divinity. The first occurrence falls in a passage where we hear the crusader admit having made a mistake in assuming that by taking the cross he would confirm his thoughts irreversibly in God's service:

Dô wânde ich sie ze gote alsô bestaeten,
daz si iemer vuoz ûz sîme dienste mêr getraeten.
(MF 181,17f)

[I thought I had so confirmed them in God
That they would never again depart from His service.]

Once again we encounter the idea that the taking of the cross should somehow automatically or magically bring about a desired deliverance of the crusader from his erstwhile attachment to worldly behavior. In Hausen's *'Mîn herze und mîn lîp diu wellent scheiden'* (MF 47,9), it was the heart that continued to beset the crusader after the latter had thought that by taking the cross he had freed himself from worldly entanglements ('ledic sîn von solicher swaere," 47,17). In Hartmann's *'Dem kriuze zimet wol reiner muot'* (MF 209,25) it seemed as if the putting on of "Kristes bluomen" (210,37) did indeed bring about the desired change, for the crusader claims that, until the day that he did so, his joy had never been carefree ("Mîn vröide wart nie sorgelos/ unz and die tage," 210,35f). In Johansdorf's poetry, on the other hand, some kind of change has clearly been viewed as a desideratum but not experienced. In the third stanza of Johansdorf's *'Die hinnen varn'* (MF 89,21) the crusader confesses that worry has brought him to the point of wanting to put away "kranken muot," this unsatisfactory mind-set of which he has up to now not been free. However, the end of the stanza and the poem finds him telling God (it is not an humble request) to look favorably upon ("vervâch ze guote," 90,15) his loving a woman above all the world. In Johansdorf's *'Guote liute, holt die gâbe'* (MF 94,14), the crusader's plea to *minne* to let him free until the crusade is over indicates that, here also, the crusader has felt the need to be released from distractions so that he can concentrate on the crusading matter at hand. However, his plea to *minne* for freedom is seriously undercut by his offer, if *minne* insists, to take (the same) *minne* with him to 'gotes lant" (94,33). He is thus quite willing to go on crusade with loyalties divided between war for God and love for woman.

Apparently Reinmar presents us with a portrayal similar to that of Hausen and Johansdorf. The second stanza of 181,13 begins with the crusader's complaints that his wayward thoughts are raging against him ("gedanke wellent toben," 181,24). Like the *herze* in Hausen's *'Mîn herze und mîn lîp'* (MF 47,9), his thoughts want to go back to the old ways ("wider an diu alten maere," 181,28). The crusader complains that the thoughts are making his situation very difficult:

> dem gote dem ich dâ dienen sol,
> den enhelfent sî mir niht sô loben,
> Als ichs bedörfte und ez mîn saelde waere.
> (MF 181,25-27)

[The God I am supposed to serve,
Him they are not helping me praise
As I need to, and as it would be good for me.]

Well taken is Dittrich's comment that this reference to God as "the God
whom I am supposed to be serving" does not have the ring of intimate
devotion.[101] It seems that the thoughts are being criticized for not
helping a crusader who is trying to maintain behavior suitable to the
cross ("als ez dem zeichen wol gezam," 181,14) when actually the
crusader himself apparently views God as a distant source of obligation
and "saelde." We remember that the crusader in Reinmar's *'Durch daz
ich vröide'* (MF 180,28) seemed similarly at pains to honor properly an
obligation to God as the giver of "saelden" (MF 180,33-35) without
apparently having any real inner fervor. He simply did not want to look
like a fool ("gouch") by failing to appear suitably grateful. Clearly,
such language does not indicate in either case any kind of intimate
bond between crusader and God. Perhaps the crusader's inability,
despite his strong sense of obligation and propriety, to keep his
thoughts focused on the crusade duty at hand stems from what Dittrich
terms his weak God-relationship ("dieser schwachen
Gottbezogenheit").[102]

In any case, the crusader sees himself unable to exercise any
control over his thoughts and thus turns, with a desparate prayer for
help, not to God--interestingly enough, in view of Dittrich's
observation--but to the Virgin Mary:

daz wende, muoter unde maget,
sît ichs in niht verbieten mac!
  (MF 31f)

[Prevent that, Mother and Maid,
Since I cannot forbid them to do anything.]

The crusader thus prays to Mary to supply the resistance to his *gedanke*
that he himself cannot muster. It is interesting to compare this prayer
with that in Friedrich von Hausen's *'Mîn herze und mîn lîp diu wellent
scheiden'* (MF 47,9) which, as already indicated, may be a source of
influence on Reinmar's poem. There we heard the crusader pray to God
to give the wayward heart what it wants by sending it back where it
will be (favorably) received ("dâ man dich well enpfân," MF 47, 28).
By contrast, Reinmar presents us with a crusader who, initially at least,

wants to resist his wayward thoughts, thus conducting himself properly ("als es dem zeichen wol gezam," 181,15) despite the pressure of contrary inclinations.

Given this avowed commitment to appropriate behavior, which seems a typical theme in Reinmar's poetry, one is startled to hear the crusader follow his prayer to the Virgin Mary with a swift and dramatic change in tone and viewpoint. Hardly has the crusader finished this prayer for her help against his wayward thoughts when we hear him defending their right to go where they please:

> Gedanken nu wil ich niemer gar
> verbieten--dês ir eigen lant--,
> in erloube in eteswenne dar
> und aber wider sà zehant.
> (MF 181,33-36)

> [I will never forbid my thoughts—
> It is (after all) their own country—
> From going there once in a while,
> But (they must come) back again right away.]

He thus insists on the rights of his *gedanke* to have a furlough now and then, a strictly limited furlough, to be sure, but one to which they are entitled. Thus, at base, the propriety-conscious crusader in this poem by Reinmar turns out to support his thoughts in their abandonment of the crusade just as the crusader in Hausen's poem supported his rebellious heart. While Hausen's crusader worried how his heart would fare without his protection ("dîne sorge helfen enden/ mit triuwen," 47,15f), the crusader in Reinmar's poem wants them to greet their common friends during their furlough at home:

> Sô si unser beider vriunde dort gegrüezen,
> sô kêren dan und helfen mir die sünde büezen,
> und sî in allez daz vergeben,
> swaz sî mir haben her getân.
> (MF 181,37-182,1)

> [When they have greeted their friends and mine,
> Then they (must) return and help me do penitence for sins.
> Therewith all will be forgiven
> That they have done to me up to now.]

With Hausen's *herze* as with Reinmar's *gedanke*, the metaphorical
designation of the crusader's inner self as "autonomous" being(s)
provides him the opportunity to revel in loving thoughts of home and to
express the strong desire to return there without completely
surrendering the semblance of loyalty to the Holy Cause. While Hausen
has the crusader express the *herze*'s need for his company and
protection, in Reinmar's case the crusader wants to benefit from the
very actions of his thoughts that he had prayed to the Virgin Mary to
prevent. In retrospect, then, his prayer to her appears to have been
either a desparate effort to fend off his contrary inclinations before his
final surrender to them, or else an empty gesture of (characteristic?)
superficial propriety.

All told, then, in Reinmar's poetry as with his fellow
vernacular poets discussed until now, dissent from and rebellion against
God receive surprisingly favorable treatment. Donning the sign of the
cross does not lead to a particulary impressive crusade stance. In
Hausen's poetry, the taking of the cross elicits the enthusiatically
positive support of the body ("gerne vehten," MF 47,11), but the active
opposition of the heart. In Hartmann's poetry, taking the cross provides
the crusader with ego-satisfaction at being better than unnamed
inferiors. However, it also leads to passionate and curious confessions
of strong attachment to the homeland and of past entanglements with
Dame World that have **not** disappeared without a trace. In Johansdorf's
poetry, taking the cross triggers blustery sermonizing by a crusader
who is himself considering not taking his own sermon to heart, and
who furthermore pronounces a standing invitation to worldly *minne* to
be his travelling companion to the land of God. And now in Reinmar's
poem we hear one who ceremoniously proclaims crusade joy while
himself demonstrating sadness at crusade inconvenience. Even worse
than that, Reinmar's crusader almost interrupts his prayer to the Virgin
Mary for deliverance from his rebellious thoughts with words that
champion their rebellion, and he reveals unmistakably his intention to
use that rebellion for his own purposes. In sum, in the crusade poetry of
Reinmar, as of his fellow poets, the veneration of God is neither
inspired nor inspiring.

Otto von Botenlauben

There is no historical record of Otto von Botenlauben's
participation in a crusade. What is documented is his long stay in the

Kingdom of Jerusalem where he married into a prominent family and acquired considerable possessions.[103]

The one crusade poem preserved in Botenlauben's opus, *'Waere Kristes lôn niht also süeze'* (KLD 41, XII[104]; KD 41), is transmitted only in Manuscript C. The poem cannot be dated with certainty, but is generally thought to have been composed in conjunction with the crusade of 1197 which was led by Emperor Henry VI, son of Frederick Barbarossa.[105] Jaehrling disagrees with this consensus, and dates the poem in the second decade of the thirteenth century. Jaehrling bases this proposal on Botenlauben's use of the term "himelrîche" which the crusader in the poem uses to characterize his lady.[106] Jaehrling does not explain his assertion that such bold metaphors ("kühne Metaphern") can be expected precisely at that later time. It has already become evident in this study that bold metaphors in German crusade poetry are quite at home in the twelfth century.

Botenlauben was the first known poet to treat the subject of the crusade in a *Wechsel*. The *Wechsel* is a traditional poetic form, apparently of German origin, in which a male and a female persona reflect upon each other without addressing one another directly in dialogue.[107] Since the woman's stanza will concern us mainly in our next chapter, it is convenient for us that Botenlauben has the man speak first. In this man we encounter a crusader for whom, like several we have already met, the crusade is an occasion for expressing a strong desire to remain in the homeland. In Hausen's *'Mîn herze den gelouben hât'* (MF 48,3) we heard that the departed crusader would be "noch alumbe den Rîn" (48,6) if it were not for love ("durch liebe oder durch der minne rât," 48,5). In Hartmann's *'Ich var mit iuweren hulden'* (MF 218,5) it is again only love, *minne*, presumably (but not clearly) the love of God, which can force the crusader to part from his homeland of "Vranken" (218,17-20). In Botenlauben's *'Waere Kristes lôn niht alsô süeze"* (KLD 41, XII),[108] it is "Kristes lôn" (one is reminded of Hartmann's *Kristes bluomen*), the reward of Christ (1,1), which alone can cause the crusader to leave his beloved lady. Here also, then, departure from home is quite explicitly a wrenching experience.

It sounds very much like an echo of Friedrich von Hausen's *'Mîn herze den gelouben hât'* (MF 48,3), when Botenlauben locates the residence of this lady "al umbe den Rîn" (1,5). One could also be reminded of the prayer in the same poem by Hausen when one hears Botenlauben's crusader close the stanza with the following entreaty for God's favor:

herre got, nu tuo mir helfe schîn
daz ich mir und ir erwerbe noch die hulde dîn!
(KLD 41,XII,1,6-7)

[Lord God, grant me your aid
That I may still gain your favor for myself and her!]

It is interesting to compare this prayer with others already encountered. In Hausen's *'Mîn herze und mîn lîp diu wellent scheiden,'* we heard the crusader ask God essentially to help his heart in its rebellion against the crusades (MF 47,27-28). In Johansdorf's *'Die hinnen varn'* we heard a crusader call on God to accept the fact that he will not give up the sin of loving a woman more than all the world (MF 90,11-15). Compared with such expectations addressed to God, the prayer in Botenlauben's *Wechsel* seems at first quite respectful and humble. The crusader in *'Waere Kristes lôn'* asks God for his help in gaining divine favor for himself and his lady love. Of course, one could find a little odd his praying to God on behalf of a woman whom he has just called his personal kingdom of heaven and whom, despite "Kristes lôn," he expressly does not want to leave. One could also find odd that it is God's favor ("hulde") that he wants to gain for himself and her, not God's reward (*lôn*) for crusade service as we heard in Hartmann's *'Swelch vrouwe sendet ir lieben man'* (MF 211,20). Why should this crusader see himself expressly as without God's favor? One answer might be that he has shown noticeably more enthusiasm in his devotion to his heavenly lady than to the God of the crusades whom he is expressly serving with reluctance. His prayer to God on behalf of his beloved, whom he has just praised as he has not praised God, only completes a picture of somewhat questionable crusade commitment. Perhaps he does well not to assume God's favor. And when we hear a little later the rest of this *Wechsel* in the words of his heavenly beloved, we will hear fairly strong confirmation for this sobering suspicion.

Hiltbolt von Schwangau

According to Juethe, a Hiltbolt von Schwangau is attested in eight documents between the years 1179 and 1256, that is, during the period when the German crusade poems of this study were composed.[109] Which one of the persons attested under this name is the poet, is a vexed question. Juethe himself prefers a dating that would link Hiltbolt's crusade either with that of 1190, the Third Crusade, or that of 1197 led by Emperor Henry VI.[110] Worstbrock similarly favors a "Datierungsansatz '1190-1210.'"[111] It just so happens that it is precisely during this period that no Hiltbolt von Schwangau is attested historically.

Both Juethe and Worstbrock base their datings on an impression of Hiltbolt's poetry--Juethe: "dem Charakter seiner Lieder"; Worstbrock: "Das Erscheinungsbild fast aller Lieder"[112]--which neither explains. It is thus not clear why either favors a dating during that period as opposed to, say, a dating 1221 or 1256 when a Hiltbolt von Schwangau is historically attested.[113] A Hiltbolt von Schwangau could well have participated in the crusade of 1217. And a Hiltbolt composing at this later time would also fit more comfortably with the influence of Reinmar, Heinrich von Morungen, and Walther von der Vogelweide which is evident in the poems preserved under his name. Reinmar and Morungen were composing around the year 1200--Morungen's death has been dated in 1222[114]--, Walther von der Vogelweide until about 1230. If compositions of Hiltbolt are dated in the 1190's, then it becomes difficult to allow time for the influence of these poets, which both Juethe and Worstbrock propose.[115] A later dating works out chronologically much better.

Hiltbolt von Schwangau's 'Ez ist ein reht daz ich lâze den muot' (KLD 24, XVII; KD 42) is transmitted in Manuscript C, the first stanza also in Manuscript B. God is mentioned twice in the poem. The first instance occurs near the end of the poem's second stanza where the speaker reveals that he is ready to leave love and loved ones ("minne und friunde," 2,7) for the sake of God ("dur got"). At this point in the poem, these words constitute a rather belated revelation that a crusade is at issue. In Friedrich von Hausen's 'Si darf mich des zîhen niet' (MF 45,37), the hearer/reader also finds out rather late in the poem that the speaker is a crusader.

Also like Hausen's poem, Hiltbolt's 'Ez ist ein reht' opens on the subject of worldly love, minne, but in a slightly different tone from the one to which we have become accustomed. The speaker begins, namely, by claiming the right to give up on love and to behave in keeping with his situation:

> Ez ist ein reht daz ich lâze den muot
> der mir ûf minne ie was rîche unde guot:
> ich wil gebâren als ez mir nu stât.

(KLD 24, XVII,1, 1-3)

[It is right that I desist from the attitude
That was always generous and good toward love:
I will now act in keeping with my situation.]

Just what has brought about this change of heart is not made clear. Instead, the speaker continues with generalizing attacks on *minne*. The attacks have something to do with parting, but are mounted without explanatory specifics:

owê daz minne ie daz boese ende hât!
swer sich mit staete an ir unstaete lât,
wê wie unsanfte dem ein scheiden tuot!
(KLD 24, XVII, 1,4-6)

[Alas! that love always has a bad ending!
If someone faithfully trusts her unfaithfulness,
Oh how painfully he will take his leave!]

These words of distress are followed by a line (1,7) in which the speaker reveals that it is he himself who has suffered misfortune. The next two lines, which close the stanza, do not reveal more specifics, but rather essentially recap the very general complaints already stated: joy (*liebe*) often becomes sorrow (1,8); thus how well off ("sanft") is the one who has guarded himself against it (1,8f). After this general opening, we learn in the second stanza that we are hearing a crusader. Actually, it is not easy to determine at what point this becomes clear. The stanza begins with a masterful rendition of a scene of parting. With dimmed and tearful eyes a group (of men, as it turns out) takes emotional and possibly final leave of a gathering of intimates. Women among those remaining behind see their recent happiness dashed by (the hovering threat of) death:

Nû werdent ougen vil trüebe unde rôt,
nâch lieben friunden sô lîdent si nôt
die ir dâ beitent vil lîhte iemermê.
daz leit getuot manger frouwen nu wê,
die fröide pflâgen mit liebe allez ê;
der wonne wendet nu mange der tôt.
(KLD XVII,2,1-6)

[Now there will be eyes dreary and red,
So distressed are they over dear friends
Who may well await them forever in vain.
This sorrow now afflicts many a woman
Who used to enjoy love and happiness.
Such bliss is now overturned for many by death.]

Then, as the seventh line of the first stanza brought the revelation that the speaker was actually telling about himself and his own personal experience, so also here the seventh line reveals that it is he who must now leave love and intimates:

minne unde friunde ich dur got lâzen wil.
(KLD 24, XVII, 7)

[Love and fiends I will now leave for God's sake.]

The remaining two lines of the stanza are apparently supposed to function as personal response to the call to God's service:

des dunket mich dur in niemer ze vil,
sît man uns vom im dienest gebôt.
(KLD 24, XVII, 7)

[For Him I do not consider that too much to ask
Since one has given us His command to serve]

The wording of these two lines reminds one of the crusader's cool and detached statement in Reinmar der Alte's 'Des tages dô ich daz kriuze nam' (MF 181,13) about the God whom one is **supposed** to be serving (181,25). Now clearly identified as a crusader, our speaker proclaims that leaving love and friends for God's sake does not seem an excessive sacrifice since, presumably (here the meaning is not entirely clear), it is ultimately with God that the command to serve has originated. In any case, as in Reinmar's poem, so here also God's worthiness to be served sacrificially is recognized correctly but without any real enthusiasm. This service is a reasonable and rightful duty, but it is not espoused with fervor.

God is mentioned for the second time in this poem late in the fourth stanza. The crusader begins this strophe by modifying the impression given at the beginning of the poem. No longer is there talk of his right to repudiate *minne*. On the contrary, though he did complain about his bad fortune at first, he is actually glad that the favor of his beloved was withheld from him:

> Daz ir genâde mich sô gar vergie,
> des bin ich frô unde klagtez doch ie.
> (KLD 24, XVII, 4, 1f)

> [That her favor was withheld from me,
> Of this I am happy, although I lamented it before.]

The explanation for this statement is that he would rather do without her noble love ("ir edler minne," 4,3) than for her to be worried about him while he is away (4,4f). He thus seems more sacrificial than his counterpart in Johansdorf's *'Guote liute, holt die gâbe'* (MF 94,15) who wanted and exhorted his lady to worry and pray (95,6-15). On the other hand, the prayer with which Hiltbolt's poem closes raises serious doubts about whether this crusader is actually so sacrificially enclined after all. The words of that prayer are these:

> got unser herre, dur den ich si lie,
> der günne mir des, werd iemer ein wîp
> der ûf genâde sül dienen mîn lîp,
> daz ez diu sî diu mich êrste gevie.
> (KLD 24, XVII, 4, 6-9)

> [May God our Lord, for whose sake I left her,
> Grant me this: Should there ever be a woman
> Whom I shall serve for her favor,
> May it be she who first captivated me.]

According to these lines, then, our crusader wants to have back the beloved woman whom he has apparently given up twice in the course of the poem, namely in stanza one where he turned from her in frustration, and in stanza four where he gave her up again to keep her from worrying about him while he is away on crusade. Thus his prayer seems to signal yet another major change of heart: he does not want to give her up and he wants only her.

Once again, then, we hear a crusader who struggles dutifully to carry out the required service to God, but whose attachment to worldly love weathers all opposing forces including the crusader's own attempt at a change of attitude. Here again the crusades constitute an interruption, expressly hoped to be a temporary one, an interruption of pursuits both trying and pleasurable, and which, so the crusader hopes, will be resumed not long hence as if no interruption had ever occurred.

Friedrich von Leiningen

Under this name the text of one crusade poem, '*Swes muot ze fröiden sî gestalt*' (KLD 12), is preserved in Manuscript C. According to Gisela Kornrumpf, the poet is probably to be identified with the Rhenish Count Friedrich von Leiningen who died in 1237 and who participated in the crusade led by Emperor Frederick II in 1227/1228.[116] Apart from the historical documentation of the Leiningen family, we have only the text of the poem as a possible indirect source of information about the poet.

Several features of this poem are unusual, even compared with the poems that we have encountered so far. It begins with a traditional nature entrance, *Natureingang*, used so effectively by Neidhart, whom we shall encounter later in our discussion. Except for Neidhart, Leiningen is, to my knowledge, the only medieval German poet to have used the *Natureingang* in crusade poetry, where indeed it might seem out of place. The *Natureingang* contains nothing that could lead hearers or readers to expect a crusade theme.[117]

In Leiningen's *Natureingang*, the speaker begins with a stirring praise of nature in spring. Whoever has a mind attuned to joy, he tells us, should look upon the very green forest and should observe how marvelously (the pursonified month of) May has clothed her retinue (presumably meaning flowers and foliage). The phrase about the birds being offended by mourning ("den vogeln trûren leidet," KLD 12,1,6) is probably an adumbration of the crusade theme that has not yet been announced at this point. If so, it is an odd reference indeed. For while the natural inclination of the birds away from sadness (*trûren*) and toward joy (*fröide*) is shared by several of our crusaders, for whom crusading is an unwelcome interruption in a life of *fröide*, none of our crusaders til now has gone so far as to call mourning hurtful ("leidet").

The first of four occurrences of God's name in this poem comes in the second stanza. This strophe, in which there is no reference to the crusade theme, is a cleverish but perhaps all too typical courtly lover's lament. The speaker complains (proudly?) that his heart will pay a toll on joy ("von fröiden gît mîn herze zol," 2,1) for as long as the one who has his heart under her control withholds her greeting. God has formed her ("gebildet," 2,6) so that the crusader's heart and his whole mind ("al mîn sin," 2,8) could not imagine how she could be more beautiful. Unfortunately, as he points out in the stanza's closing line, she is also the one who wants to reduce his joy ("fröide krenken," 2,11). Thus, God is first mentioned in reference to a complaint to the effect that, by creating this woman, God has done the crusader at best a very dubious favor if not a plain disservice. This statement echoes the question in Friedrich von Hausen's 'Sî darf mich des zîhen niet' (MF 45,37) why God created the woman so beautiful ("sô rehte wol getân," 46,18) if love for woman can be sin to the crusader on duty.

The third stanza of Leiningen's poem is a prayer. We have encountered repeated cases of oddly placed and peculiarly formulated prayers in connection with potentially sinful amorous affection. Leiningen's case is something of a new departure since the crusader in his poem does not pray to God, but rather to the sweet counselor Love ("Minne, süeziu râtgebîn," 3.1). As curious as this may be, however, essentially Leiningen is merely demonstrating openly a sentiment that has been latent, and often not so latent, in all the crusader portrayals that we have encountered so far, with the possible (but by no means certain) exception of Hartmann von Aue. Love has consistently been in control, and God has repeatedly been either asked or presumed to provide services that have nothing to do with either His traditional orthodox representation or His traditional role as Lord of the crusades. And in none of these crusader portrayals has God been the recipient of the kind of fervent prayer that is addressed to Love in this stanza:

> Ach Minne, süeziu râtgebîn,
> rât, daz du saelic müezest sîn,
> mîns herzen küeneginne,
> rât daz si mir tuo helfe schîn,
> rât daz si wende mînen pîn,
> vil minneclîchiu Minne.
> sît du slôz bist unde bant
> mîns herzen und der sinne,
> sô râtâ, jâ dest an der zît:
> mîn trôst, mîn heil gar an dir lît,
> in dîner gluot ich brinne.
>   (KLD 12,3)

> [Oh, Love, sweet counselor,
> I will bless you if you
> Advise the queen of my heart.

Advise her to come to my aid,
Advise her to relieve my pain,
O excellent Love.
Since you are the lock and cinch
Of my heart and mind,
So counsel, it is high time.
My comfort and salvation lie entirely in you,
I am burning in your embers.]

Here at last is the fervent prayer of devotion with cry for succor to an
ardently cherished divinity to whom the petitioner is profoundly
committed. It is the kind of prayer which we have up to now heard **no**
crusader address either to God (Father, Son, or Holy Spirit) or to the
Virgin Mary. This crusader's comfort and salvation ("trôst" and "heil")
rests in earthly love, not in the heavenly God.

It is the fourth stanza that finally introduces the crusade theme,
a delayed introduction which we have already encountered several
times. Strictly speaking, the crusade is not explicitly mentioned at all,
and in fact by simply presupposing its presence and not arguing for it at
any length, I am taking advantage of a perhaps facile scholarly
consensus. The speaker merely laments that he must depart from his
beloved and take the road to Apulia[118]:

ôwe der leiden verte
die dann gen Pülle tuot mîn lîp,
    (12,4 3-40)

[Alas for the sorrowful trip
That I will take to Apulia!]

This fourth stanza also introduces a theme which will be of more direct
concern in the next chapter of this study. However, it must be dealt
with now in some measure since it cannot be separated from the last
two occurrences of God--one actually of Christ--in Leiningen's poem.
In the next lines following his revelation that he must travel to Apulia,
the crusader immediately addresses his beloved with the peculiar
request that she not be so severe toward him (4,5-6). Why should he
expect callous treatment precisely in this hour of apparent special need
for her support? And his request is repeated in the next lines where he
asks her to temper her mood and to lift his spirits by giving her blessing
on his travel (4,7-11).

Kornrumpf's comment about this blessing, which opens the fifth stanza, as characterized by "aller Johansdorfschen Innigkeit der Frauenstrophe"[119] is probably more pertinent than her generalizing formulation indicates. For there are solid reasons for seeing Leiningen's final stanza as patterned on the fourth and likewise final stanza of Albrecht von Johansdorf's *'Guote liute, holt die gâbe'* (MF 94,15). Strictly speaking, however, in this **fourth** stanza of Johansdorf's poem one encounters neither "Inningkeit" nor "Frauenstrophe." The **third** stanza of Johansdorf's poem, which is indeed a *Frauenstrophe*, will concern us in the next chapter of this study. Suffice it here to note briefly that Johansdorf's poem is a *Wechsel*, a form in which, as noted previously, man and woman utter speeches that are interrelated without actually engaging in dialogue.

The woman speaking in the *Frauenstrophe* of Johansdorf's *Wechsel* laments bitterly her beloved crusader's departure and asks herself how she is going to behave ("wie wil du dich gebâren," 94,39) when he is gone, and how she is going to survive in the world and in her despondence ("Wie sol ich der werlde und mîner klage geleben?" 95,2). Thus Leiningen's poem is like Johansdorf's in that the crusader in both cases must deal, as part of his preparations for departure, with a beloved woman who makes that departure more difficult by objecting to it vehemently and without reserve.

In Johansdorf's final stanza, the crusader utters a blessing upon his beloved as if she were the supportive woman called for in Hartmann von Aue's *'Swelch vrowe sendet ir lieben man'* (MF 211,20) even though the female persona in *'Guote liute, holt die gâbe,'* as elsewhere in Johansdorf's crusade songs, is consistently the opposite of this supportive woman. Moreover, Johansdorf's crusader elaborates further his daydream of woman supporting crusader by imagining her praying on his behalf while he carries her in his heart across the sea. This passage from Johansdorf's poem reads as follows:

> Wol si, saelic wîp,
> diu mit ir wîbes güete gemachen kan,
> daz man si vüeret über sê.
> ir vil guote lîp
> den sol er loben, swer ie herzeliep gewan,
> wande ir heime tuot alsô wê
> Swenne sî gedenket an sîne nôt.
> 'lebt mîn herzeliep oder ist er tôt,'
> sprichet sî, 'sô müeze sîn pflegen,

dur den er süezer lîp sich dirre welte hât bewegen.'
(MF 95,6-15)

[Bless her, glorious woman
Whose womanly goodness can cause one
To carry her over the sea.
She deserves the praise
Of everyone who has ever known true love,
For at home she suffers so
When she thinks about his distress.
'Whether my beloved is alive or dead,'
She says, 'He must care for him
For Whose sake he left this (part of) the world.']

Thus, in a fit of wishful thinking, Johansdorf's crusader **imagines** his beloved praying on his behalf, an action which--let it be repeated--does not take place and is indeed totally out of character for the woman as **portrayed** in Johansdorf's crusade poems. There are no portrayals of praying woman in medieval German crusade poetry.

Leiningen treats a situation so similar that Kornrumpf surely has good reason to sense a connection. His crusader also faces the displeasure of a beloved woman who confronts him pointedly with her objections to his departure. The passage in question, which also ends Leiningen's poem, reads as follows:

senfte ein kleine dînen muot
und sprich ûz rôtem munde
zuo mir niht wan eht fünf wort,
diu hoehent mîner fröiden hort:
'var hin ze guoter stunde!'
'In guoter stunde sî dîn vart,
dîn lîp dîn sêle sî bewart,
dîn lop dîn heil dîn êre!
mac dichs niht wenden mîn gebot
mîn flê mîn dröu, daz weiz wol got,
sô wil ich biten sêre,
sît daz dîn vart unwendic ist,
zwei herze in arebeite,
daz mîn und dîn, du füerest hin,
dâ von ich iemer trûric bin:
nu sî Krist dîn geleite!'
(KLD 12, 4,7 - 5,11)

[Temper your mood a little
And let your red lips
Speak only these five words to me
Which shall heighten my joy:
'Go under a good aegis!'
'Under a good aegis may your travel be,
And may your body and soul be protected,
And your praise, your salvation and your honor!
If my command cannot stop you,
Nor my begging, nor my threatening, God knows,
So I will plead with you fervently:
Since your travel is irreversible,
Take with you two hearts in heaviness,
Mine and your's,
Which will make me sad forever.
Now may Christ be your guide!]

While Johansdorf's crusader **imagined** his beloved thinking supportively about him and praying on his behalf, here in Leiningen's poem the crusader **petitions** his beloved **directly** for her support and asks her specifically for a parting blessing. His plea that his beloved lady not be so severe toward him ("wis gen mir niht sô herte," 4,6) evokes the kind of resistance to his departure that we shall shortly hear the woman in Johansdorf's *Wechsel* actually utter.

At this point, Leiningen proceeds differently from Johansdorf in a basic and important way. Namely, while Johansdorf had the crusader imagine support and prayer of his beloved that are out of character with the portrayal of woman in his poetry, Leiningen portrays the crusader's beloved in his poem as actually responding in her own words. To his request for the five words of blessing which he formulates for her, she reponds immediately with a blessing whose initial line echoes his request. However, she continues by making clear her strong opposition to what is happening. Thus while Johansdorf has his crusader downplay his beloved's opposition to his commitment, Leiningen elaborates the female opposition by having her spell it out. She tells the departing crusader in no uncertain terms that by leaving he is going against her orders, her pleas, and her threats (5,4-5). It is striking that she calls on God as a witness to her exasperation (5,5). And it is quite peculiar that she asks the crusader, since his travel cannot be prevented, to take with him two hearts in distress, something that will leave her ever forlorn (5,7-10). Why does she ask him to take both hearts? Why should he not leave his heart with her as the familiar tradition requires and as is suggested in the poem by the Burggraf von Lienz discussed next in this study? And how is one to understand the closing line of the poem in which she invokes upon him the guidance of Christ. There is something odd about the tone of these words. Plausible would be an intonation of anger or sarcasm. This final blessing is hardly an expression of intimacy and inspiration, for the signs of her displeasure are much too clear and unmistakable. These are the words of a woman who is staunchly but futilely anti-crusade. God is her witness.

Der Burggraf von Lienz

This poet belonged to a family of *ministeriales* of Lienz (Lüenz) who lived on the Drau (Drava) River in the Carinthian district of present-day Austria.[120] The leading candidate is Burggraf *Heinric* who appears in documents between 1231 and 1269. The crusade in question is thought to be that of 1227-1228 led by Emperor Frederick II, in which it is also assumed that Friedrich von Leiningen participated.

The crusade theme is treated in one of two poems that appear under Lienz's name, and specifically in the loosely attached final strophe of '*Ez gienc ein juncfrou minneclîch*' (KLD 36, I; KD 66), transmitted in Manuscript C. This poem is composed in a combination of genres. It begins as a *Serena*, in which, after hearing a lady's instructions to a watchman in preparation for the secret arrival of her lover, we experience that arrival itself. The poem continues as a dawn song (*Tagelied*), in which is depicted the passionate and painful parting of the lovers after their night together.[121] Thus the crusade theme appears in surroundings which are perhaps even less appropriate for that theme than the *Natureingang* and the prayer to *Minne râtgebîn* in Friedrich von Leiningen's '*Swes muot ze fröiden sî gestalt.*'

The name of God occurs three times in the six verses of Lienz's *Serena*-plus-*Tagelied*-plus-crusade song.[122] It appears first at the end of stanza three in the last line of the woman's words of parting. Since at this point there has been no indication of the coming crusade theme, there is nothing particularly unusual about her words of farewell. They do provide an interesting point of contrast with the words uttered in a similar situation by the woman in Leiningen's '*Swes muot ze fröiden sî gestalt.*' For while in the latter the woman commissioned her departing crusader to take with him both her and his sorrowful hearts, here in Lienz's '*Ez gienc ein juncfrou minneclîch*' the woman proposes the more traditional exchange of hearts whereby she will keep his, and hers will go with him. And while Leiningen had the woman let her crusader know very pointedly that by leaving he was clearly disregarding her wishes, Lienz has the woman resist her lover's departure less outspokenly, though not without signs of displeasure on her own part. Finally, while the closing words of Leiningen's poem, on the surface an invoking of God's blessings on the crusader, may well have been, at least in part, a covert venting of bitterness, the woman in Lienz's blesses her beloved less ambiguously, but follows that blessing, as her last word, with a clear expression of her objection to his leaving. Her words of parting read as follows:

> 'du lâ mich dir bevolhen sîn
> als du mir bist für alle man:
> bî mir hân ich daz herze dîn,
> des mînen ich dir vil wol gan.
> Dem hôhsten gote bevilhe ich dich.
> Ein scheiden von dir riuwet mich.'
> (KLD 36,I,4,5-10)

> [Let me be commended to you
> As you are to me above all men;
> I have your heart with me,
> And I would gladly have you take mine.
> I commend you to the highest God.
> Parting from you grieves me.]

Thus the woman's opposition to her beloved's departure is expressed here in a tone that is strikingly subdued and plaintive. We hear pain and resignation instead of outrage and bitterness. Still, her opposition is clear and unmistakable.

The remaining two occurrences of God's name come in the sixth and final stanza, which no longer belongs to the initial fiction of the poem. That fiction ended in stanza five with the passionate and painful separation typical of the dawn song. An accompanying general statement notes that joy is often followed by sorrow (5,9), followed by the narrative report (5,10) that the lover departed happy ("gemeit").

In the sixth stanza a departing crusader (the same man?) reports that the time is approaching that he must (also?) depart. How shall he leave his friends ("friunde," 6,2), he continues, without having had a chance to extend to them a parting greeting. He tells us the greeting that he would have extended had he had the opportunity. It reads as follows:

> daz ir der hôhste müeze pflegen!
> ich hân gedingen in daz lant
> dâ got vil menschlich inne gie.
> wer seit in wider uf den Sant
> dâ ich die lieben alle lie,
> und ich kein urloup von in habe?
> mîn wille stêt ze Kristes grabe.
> (KLD I,6,4-10)

> [May the Highest care for them!
> I am set to go to the land
> Where God walked in human form.
> Who will tell those on the Sant
> Where I left all my loved ones
> From whom I have not taken leave?
> My will is set toward Christ's grave.]

Thus a poem which begins as perhaps the most worldly of traditional forms, the erotic meeting and parting of furtive lovers, ends in a very realistic atmosphere of leave-taking from loved ones and with an expression of determination to press on in a spirit of firm crusade commitment. It is not clear what has hindered the crusader from saying goodbye to his intimates. It is interesting that his loved ones are mentioned as a group in which no specific person is singled out. Von Kraus's conjecture that the plural *friunde* refers surreptitiously to the one beloved[123] reminds us of passages encountered earlier in this study; here, however, the clear plural forms ("die lieben alle," 6,8; "in," 6,9) together with the totally unerotic tone of the stanza speak against that conjecture. We remember also the group of intimates portrayed so effectively in Leiningen's *'Swes muot ze fröiden sî gestalt.'* As there the realistic group scene of crusade parting stood at considerable tension with the focus on the loving couple, so here the final likewise realistic parting of a single crusader relates at best very tenuously to the 'furtive love' theme in the preceding *Serena* and dawn song. It is not clear that it is related at all.

In any case, we do hear in Lienz's poem a crusader and a woman speak of God and to God in a manner that is in keeping with traditional expectations. The woman's blessing on her departing beloved ("dem hôhsten gote bevilhe ich dich", 4,9) has the ring of impeccable orthodoxy. The same can be said for the crusader's pious references to the Holy Land in the final stanza; we hear this kind of language here for the first time in the portrayal of a crusader. It seems all the more peculiar, therefore, that such impeccable crusade references to God and His land should appear at the end of a poem belonging to a genre that by definition features the portrayal of adulterous worldly love.

Interim Summary: The Crusader and God

Even in Latin crusade poetry, as we noted earlier, the case of God as a crusade topic is a striking one due to a noteworthy historical development. In the poems composed before the Battle of Hattin, God received little attention in Latin crusade poetry apparently because there was no profound sense of need for Him. Amid the joyous celebration of the capture of Jerusalem and its anniversaries, God is mentioned rarely, sometimes receiving clearly less glory than earthly rulers (e.g., KL 4). In the poem *'Exsurgat gens Christiana'* (KL 7), in which the warlike qualities of the Germans are praised highly, God is not mentioned at all.

After Hattin, however, God becomes the major focus of Latin crusade poems which now dwell consistently on penitence and faith. In such poems as *'Iuxta trenos Ieremie'* (KL 10), *'Quod spiritu David precinuit'* (KL 16), and *'Miror, cur tepeat'* (KL 20) we encounter a profound and intense religiosity, unheard in the poems before Hattin, in which penitence and faith have become more important than weapons and martiality. To be sure, there are also poems, such as *'Plange, Sion et Iudaea'* (KL 12), Erbo's *'Indue cilicium'* (KL 15), and *'Diro satis percussus vulnere'* (KL 25) in which God is blamed and criticized for incomprehensibly allowing Christian calamities. And there are even at least two poems, namely *'Crucifigat omnes'* (KL 13) and Philip the Chancellor's (fragmentary?) *'Venit Jesus in propria'* (KL 17), in which God appears helpless or in need of human help. Nevertheless, though the concerns addressed to Him or expressed for him vary considerably, after the Christian defeat at Hattin God becomes in Latin crusade poetry the main focus of almost every poem.

Precisely during this period when God as a subject comes to dominate crusade poems in Latin, the recorded history of German crusade poetry begins. And here God is from the beginning a much more modest and a very different presence. On the whole, our crusader portrayals do not contain a great deal about God. Friedrich von Hausen's poems render God incidental to the worldly concerns of *minne*. In the poetry of Hartmann von Aue, the crusade provides an opportunity for the demonstration of superior knightly qualities while God himself serves as garantor of suitable reward (and of damnation for the weak and disloyal). Albrecht von Johansdorf depicts conflict between perceived duty to God and worldly *minne*, and indicates unmistakably that God will have to live with this conflict: *minne* has a standing invitation to accompany the crusader to Palestine. Reinmar der Alte presents God as the source of blessings toward Whom the crusader feels indebted and obligated to behave with propriety, but, in point of fact, as a very distant source of Whom the crusader speaks with patent detachment. Otto von Botenlauben designates the lady as the heaven of a crusader who has left her with emphatic reluctance for the reward of Christ ("Kristes lôn"). Hiltbolt von Schwangau depicts a crusader who faces duty less reluctantly as a rightful obligation ("niemer ze vil"), but one placed upon him through a strikingly indirect and impersonal command; by contrast this crusader becomes very direct and personal with God when he prays for a chance to serve his beloved (again). And in the poem of Friedrich von Leiningen, while God is praised as the creator of a woman who could not be more beautiful, the crusader's only prayer is not to God, but to "Minne, sueziu râtgebîn." Here we also hear, for the first time, the voice of woman asking God's blessing on her departing crusader beloved, albeit a blessing uttered in closest juxtaposition to expressions of displeasure with his going. We hear a second blessing in the poem of the Burggraf von Lienz, where it takes place in a typical dawn-song parting at the end of an adulterous assignation.

Thus while in Latin crusade poetry after Hattin God is clearly the main focus of attention and of intense and various concerns, in the contemporaneous crusade poems in German, God is consistently upstaged by other worldly cares that have to do usually with earthly love. God in German crusade poetry is clearly not the awe-inpiring object of fervent requests and intense feelings that He is in Latin crusade poems. And in some cases, God is clearly a subsidiary factor commanding the personal interest and involvement of the crusader, even in prayer, clearly less than does worldly love.

4. The Crusader and Woman

In Part II our study will focus on the female *persona*, the **portrayal** of the woman in medieval German crusade poetry. Here in this section we will take a close look at the woman **as seen through the eyes of the crusader** portrayed in the poems. How would the latter have the woman behave during this time of painful partings and stressful uncertainties? How does he see her behaving? The answers to these questions are perceptible with varying explicitness in the poems under discussion.

In the case of Friedrich von Hausen, only one stanza of one poem addresses this question directly.[124] In the second stanza of '*Mîn herze den gelouben hât*' (MF 48,3; KD 25), the speaker calls upon good ladies ("guoten vrowen," 48,13) to refrain from romances with any man who does not have the nerve to go on crusade ("der gotes verte alsô erschrac," 48,18). This call is probably echoed by Hartmann von Aue's '*Swelch vrowe sendet ir lieben man*' (MF 211,20; KD 37) which gives the similar but more positive advice that a woman should be the inspiration and support for her man's crusade participation, promising her reward if she carries out her role of home support in the required fashion. Reinmar der Alte, who was familiar with the poetry of Hausen and perhaps also with that of Hartmann, has the crusader in '*Durch daz ich vröide hie bevor ie gerne pflac*' (MF 180,28; KD 40) speak even more positively when he proclaims confidently that the sensible and honorable woman ("diu sinne und êre hât," 181,8) will not fall prey to crusade shirkers who expect to benefit from the absence of men fulfilling their crusading obligations.

It is not fully clear how these statements about women are to be understood. The warning against unworthy men addressed to good women in Hausen's '*Ich gunde es guoten vrowen niet*' (48,13; KD 25) is strikingly shrill. Could these be words of desparation in the face of an inevitable occurrence? The exhortation to women in Hartmann's '*Swelch vrowe sendet ir lieben man*' (MF 211,20; KD 37) is less shrill but is essentially the same (futile?) warning to women against misbehavior (211,23f). And when we hear in Reinmar's '*Durch daz ich vröide hie bevor ie gerne pflac*' (MF 180,28; KD 40) the expression of confidence that dishonorable men will not have their way with women of honor and sensibility, we dare not forget that we are listening to a crusader prone to self-contradiction and thus of limited credibility.

Our caution can only be underscored by the unsettling view of woman in Johansdorf's '*Ich und ein wîp*' (MF 87,29; KD 30). Here we hear a crusader proclaim that he will continue to praise his lady on his voyage however strong the sea and waves may rage (87,37f); on the other hand, he does not expect her to behave the same way:

> der donreslege mohte aber lîhte sîn,
> dâ si mich dur lieze.
> (MF 88,1f)

> [However, there could easily be thunderbolts
> That would cause her to leave me.]

In direct contrast to his example of steadfastness, he expects her to be easily moved to betrayal.

The crusader in '*Waere Kristes lôn niht alsô süeze*' (KLD 41, XII; KD 41) is the first to be portrayed as speaking concretely about his beloved. He informs us that if it were not for the reward of Christ ("Kristes lôn") he would not have left his beloved lady "al umbe den Rîn" (1,5). Thus the crusader speaks openly about the tension between his crusading duty to Christ and devotion to his beloved on the Rhine, whom he boldly characterizes as his kingdom of heaven, his "himelrîche" (1,4). It is here that we hear for the first time a crusader speak clearly about his lady as an individual personality and discuss her in the context of his crusade obligation. It is interesting that he expresses no desire for her support of him on crusade and no expectations of her devotion and faithfulness, as we heard them in the poetry of Hausen, Hartmann, and Reinmar. Instead, the implication of the crusader's prayer to God is that he will try to win God's favor on behalf of both his "heavenly" beloved and himself. No expectations of her are mentioned.

The crusade poem of Hiltbolt of Schwangau, '*Ez ist ein reht daz ich lâze den muot*' (KLD 24, XVII; KD 42) begins with the crusader's lengthy complaint about the inconstancy of *minne* in which he makes no mention of his beloved. In fact, the beloved does not appear until the poem's fourth and final stanza. And with the fourth line of this stanza begins the very striking passage where we heard the crusader express happiness that his love has remained unrequited, since he prefers to suffer rejection from his beloved than to have her worry about him while he is on crusade. Still, he prays to God asking that if success in love is ever granted him, it should be with the same woman.

Thus, as in the case of Otto von Botenlauben, the crusader as portrayed by Hiltbolt von Schwangau also makes no reference to any crusade obligations on the part of his beloved. On the contrary, he is at pains to shelter her from the concern about him that is demanded of women, or at least expected, according to the poetry of Hartmann von Aue.

In '*Swes muot ze fröiden sî gestalt*' (KLD 12) by Friedrich von Leiningen, the ladylove of the crusader is only introduced in the last two stanzas of the poem, stanzas four and five, together with the crusade theme. These stanzas reveal essentially nothing about the crusader's view of his lady, or at best indirectly. We find him in an attitude of defensiveness because of her strong objections to his enlistment. His only expressed wish is that she will temper her anger enough to grant him a parting word of blessing. Otherwise, it is clear that his action has aroused her considerable displeasure.

Finally, in "*Ez gienc ein juncfrou minneclich*' by Der Burggraf von Lienz (KLD 36, I; KD 66), the crusade theme is completely separated from the female presence in the poem. For while the woman is the actual star of the *Serena* and dawn song (*Tagelied*) which constitute the first five of the poem's six stanzas, in stanza six, the only one in which the crusade theme appears, there is no mention of a woman, but only of a collective of "friunde" (6,2) and "lieben." Lienz keeps his treatment of woman and *minne* separate from his treatment of the crusade, and one has the feeling that this is done quite consciously and carefully.

Interim Summary: The Crusader and Woman

For the topic of woman, Latin crusade poetry offers no point of comparison since there is essentially no discussion of women in these poems. Even the Virgin Mary is mentioned in only one Latin poem, namely in '*Quomodo cantibimus*' (KL 18), while she is refered to in two medieval German crusade songs, namely as "gotes muoter" (MF 90,2) in Albrecht von Johansdorf's '*Die hinnen varn*' (KD 27) and as "muoter unde maget" (MF 181,31) in Reinmar der Alte's '*Des tâges dô ich daz kriuze nam*' (KD 39).

However, even in German crusade poetry references to the earthly woman are not plentiful, nor are they particularly flattering. In fact, the view of woman in these poems is fraught with tension and dichotomy. On the one hand, some earlier poems expressly call upon woman to remain faithful to her departed crusader in his absence, therewith implying, of course, that her faithfulness in not self-evident. In addition, where there is an explicit indication in the words of the crusader being portrayed (e.g., Johansdorf), it is clear that woman's capability for faithfulness is not highly regarded in his estimation. This view from the man's perspective of woman in conjunction with the crusade becomes all the more intriguing in comparison with those poems in which the woman is portrayed. For here, as we learn in the next section, the woman's support for the crusades is simply not an option. In crusade poetry where the woman herself is directly portrayed, her voice is exclusively the voice of opposition.

Summary of Part I: Portraying The Crusader In Medieval German Poetry

Four topics have guided our discussion of how the crusader is portrayed in medieval German poetry: Jerusalem, the enemy, God, and woman. Of the four, Jerusalem and the enemy play almost no role in these portrayals. The third topic, God, is curiously understated in contrast to contemporary Latin crusade poetry where God's role becomes prominent precisely around the time when the German poems begin to be transmitted. The fourth topic, woman, is not an issue in Latin crusade poetry. Given the probability that the authors of these poems were clerics, this will hardly be a surprise, although it is also not totally self-evident when one considers the prominent role of woman in medieval Latin poetry generally (e.g., in the *Carmina Burana*). The fact is, however, that woman is also not a very substantial presence in German poetry portraying the crusader.

All four topics—Jerusalem, the enemy, God, and woman—are dealt with in ways that surprise and intrigue. The crusader in these poems calls upon God almost exclusively in regard to worldly concerns, usually having to do with worldly love (*minne*). Meanwhile, woman also does not make an impressive showing in these crusader portrayals: while serving in a few cases as a troubling distraction from crusade duty (Hausen, Johansdorf), in other cases she is the object either of instructions, warnings, complaints, or suggestions indicating something less than the highest regard for her strength of character.

Thus the crusaders portrayed in medieval German literature do not display a great deal of interest in Jerusalem, the enemy, God, or the beloved woman. Essentially, medieval German crusade poetry focuses on a few stock situations in a framework that is used with striking repetition: the primary focus is on the mentality of the crusader who, whether about to depart or already underway, is torn between crusade duty and personal inclination. The focus is almost exclusively on the inner self. Only a few later poets (e.g., Hiltbolt von Schwangau) provide brief glances at the circumstances of departure. Overall, this is not a poetry designed to represent the crusader's lived experience.

What we have encountered, rather, is poetry as an expression of discomfort, of scarcely veiled doubt and indecision, of the love of home, and of the pain of parting from homeland and intimates. These poems are dominated by the ardent complaints of men who have enlisted in an undertaking for which enthusiasm is viewed as appropriate but difficult to muster. These are poems about recruits who do not really care about the Holy Land or the "pagan" enemy who holds it captive. What they do care about is home and the inner struggles triggered by their confrontation with the necessity of departing from it.

As such, the portrayal of the crusader in medieval German poetry fits well into what we know of the reality of the times. For the poems that have come down to us were composed in an age of widespread opposition to the crusades in Europe.[125] This opposition coincided with the end of a shift from the broad-based impetus of the first crusade spearheaded by the French nobility[126] to the top-down version of the mid-to-later 12th century, led by popes, emperors, and illustrious kings.[127]

This reflection of reality is, however, not to be understood as a turn to realism, as an "Einbruch der Kreuzzugs-Wirklichkeit," in the sense of Wentzlaff-Eggbert.[128] We have already noted that the portrayal of the crusader in medieval German poetry provides precious little information about the details of this involvement and features a pronounced lack of interest in the realities of the crusade experience. Instead, this portrayal focuses mainly on the inner life of the crusader in a few situations, particularly the situation of departure, which are treated so similarly in the works of several poets that coincidence is unlikely. Again, comparison with the much more detailed and varied settings of Latin crusade poetry serve to set these limits in bold relief. The limited and repetitive focus of medieval German crusade poetry is undoubtedly limitation with a purpose. To this point we will return later in the study.

In the meantime, let it be suggested tentatively that the medieval German poems that we have read so far are best understood as imaginative reflections of the response to the pressures felt by some sectors of lay society as that society was called upon to bear the burden of onerous and perilous travel to a dangerous war. The lack of interest in Jerusalem and the enemy, and the curiously restrained and even defensive attitude towards God fit well into this picture. This is the poetry of lay circles, which, while preferring to stay in the beloved homeland, see themselves obligated to respond suitably to the call for distant travel and myriad dangers in the service of God and crusade.

PART II.
The Female Persona In
Medieval German Crusade Poetry

Prelude: The Female Persona In Poems Of Marcabru And Guiot de Dijon

There is a small group of medieval poems in Occitan, Old French, and Middle High German in which a female speaker reacts to a crusade.[129] In each case the woman's reaction is a negative one. To my knowledge, there is no medieval poem in which a female persona speaks in support of a crusade. Meanwhile, we have already encountered a poem by Albrecht von Johansdorf in which a male speaker imagines a woman speaking in favor of a crusade; we shall shortly hear a second example by Heinrich von Rugge. And, of course, we have already noted poems by Hausen, Hartmann, and Johansdorf, and Leiningen in which a male crusader calls for the woman's support of crusade or crusader. In medieval German poetry, at least, male pressure for woman's support of the crusades stands side by side with female resistance and opposition.

Before turning to the medieval German examples, it will prove helpful to look briefly at two well-known Romance crusade poems featuring a female persona. The earliest of these is '*A la fontana del vergier*' (KD 11) by the Occitan poet Marcabru.[130] In this poem, which Taylor dates "sometime after Easter 1147,"[131] a woman identified as the daughter of a castle lord ("Filha d'un senhor de castelh," II, 9) is approached by an unidentified admirer who wishes to replace in her favor the beloved crusader whose absence she is grieving. In the course of warding off this "unprincipled seducer,"[132] our heroine is heard to rail against Jesus ("vostra anta mi cofon," III, 18) for taking from her the best man in all the world (III, 20), and at King Louis ("mala fos reys Lozoicx," IV, 26) for authorizing crusade calls and sermons. She also prays to the Lord ("Senher") in the last stanza of the poem for mercy in the next life where she will presumably be safe from the clutches of lecherous opportunists such as the one who has sought her out.

The other Romance example is the Old French poem *'Chanterai por mon corage'* (KD 22) composed probably in the late 12th century by Guiot de Dijon.[133] Here also a woman beset with concern for a crusader facing the ferocious Saracens rebukes God, asking Him why he has separated two people, both very good looking, who love each other:

> S'il est biaus et je sui gente.
> Sire, por quoi le feis?
> Quant l'uns a l'autre atalente,
> Por coi nos en departis?
> (III, 29-32)

> [If he is handsome and I am fair
> Lord, why did you do this?
> Since we hold one another dear,
> Why did you separate us?]

These two poems are remarkably similar on the point at issue: two women worried about beloved crusaders gone overseas to face a dangerous enemy express displeasure at God concerning their distress. The similarity between the two Romance poems is all the more remarkable given the (very little) information that is available to us about the two poets. While there have been occasional attempts to upgrade his status, it seems evident that Marcabru was a "troubadour plébeien"[134] of "the humblest origins"[135] who made his living as a traveling minstrel (*joglar*).[136] We know nothing certain about Guiot de Dijon, but a reasonably plausible guess is that he was a "protegé" of a lord of Chacenay in Bourgogne,[137] thus perhaps a member of the lower (middle?) nobility, but probably not a minstrel of low birth. Thus two poets from different time periods, different areas, and probably from different levels of social status at some point in their careers gave voice to woman's discomfort with the crusade and to her displeasure with God concerning that discomfort. The poems of several medieval German poets (coincidentally?) echo that sentiment.

The Female Persona in Medieval German Crusade Poems

Albrecht von Johansdorf

Two poems by Johansdorf, both of which we encountered above, depict a woman affected by the crusade. *'Mich mac der tôt von ir minnen wol scheiden'* (MF 87,5; KD 28) is a narrative with dialogue in which a recently enlisted crusader relates his being confronted by his lady with objections to his enlistment. *'Guote liute, holt die gâbe'* (MF 94,15; KD 29) is a *Wechsel,* a poetic form in which man and woman express themselves about each other without actually addressing each other directly. Here the woman gives vent to her distress about her crusader's departure and its implications for her life.

In the former poem, the crusader prefaces his report of the confrontational conversation with a declaration of his love for the woman whom he has chosen for his joy ("ze einer vröide erkorn," 87,8). Only death can separate her from his love (87,5f). He swears that he is cursed before God as a heathen if he deservedly provokes her anger (87,9f), an oath which will turn out to anticipate the anger that he will actually encounter.

At the beginning of the second stanza, the crusader reports the scene in which his lady fair ("diu wolgetâne") notices his wearing the sign of the cross (87,13f). She opens the dialogue by asking him the following pointed question:

'Wie wiltu nû geleisten diu beide,
varn über mer und iedoch wesen hie?
(MF 87,15f)

[How do you propose to do both these things:
Travel overseas and still be here?]

At this climactic point, unfortunately, a problem in transmission has resulted in the loss of probably two lines.[138] It is clear, in any case, that the tense encounter does not take a positive turn, for in the one line of the stanza remaining after the textual corruption, we hear the crusader wail that he was in pain before, but that now the situation has worsened: "ê was mir wê: dô geschach mir nie sô leide" (87,20).

The crusader's response to this heated query of his beloved is strikingly threadbare and incoherent. His attempt at an answer is an incommunicative jumble of trappings from crusade sermons. Don't be too sad, he tells her (87,21), since we are going to the Holy Grave to fight for God's honor ("dur des rîchen gotes êre," 87,22). Whoever stumbles there ("bestrûchet"), may fall ("besnaben," 87,25). And the souls will be happy when they enter heaven in style ("mit schallen," 87,28). The text does not hang together. Editorial conjectures indicate a game but futile struggle to make it cohere. It is very likely that some incoherence is intended by the author: The crusader's words of response to his beloved, with which the poem closes, do not and indeed can not provide a direct answer to her very direct but unanswerable question.

The voice of the woman is also heard in the *Wechsel 'Guote liute, holt die gâbe'*(MF 94,15). In this poem the crusader begins by exhorting good people to go and fetch the gift which God himself gives. The opening of this poem reminds one of Marcabru's crusade poem *'Pax in nomine Domini'* (Dejeanne XXXV; KD 10)[139] in which potential crusaders are enjoined to go and enjoy the bath ("lavador," I,6; II,6 and IV,6) that God has prepared for them on the battlefields of Spain.

As noted previously, Johansdorf's poem *'Guote liute'* changes its tone drastically after its sermonizing first stanza. In the second, the crusader pleads with *minne* to release him for a limited period to carry out his crusade duties, but then abruptly changes his tone and declares himself ready to take *minne* with him to "gotes lant" (94,33).

The woman's stanza is the third of this *Wechsel*. It is thus immediately preceded by the crusader's reminder to God that the good woman ("der guoten," 94,34) is due half the crusader's reward. Except for this pointed reminder, the speech of the crusader contrasts sharply with that of the woman. His words are fraught with the complexity and indecisiveness of a man torn between two impulses. Her speech is resolutely single-minded, focusing exclusively on the dire consequences of his departure:

> 'wie vil mir doch von liebe leides ist beschert!
> Waz mir diu liebe leides tuot!
> (MF 94,36f)

> ⌊How much harm is accorded me by the pleasure of love!
> What harm the pleasure of love does me!⌋

She wonders how, bereft of joy ("vröidelôser lîp," 94,38), she will conduct herself once the one is gone who always kept her in high spirits ("hôchgemuot," 95,1). How, she asks, will she live with the world and her own sadness, now that he is about to depart? Not a word in this stanza diverges from this concentrated lamentation.

The final stanza of the poem provides a study in contrast between this portrayal of woman as concerned only about her personal loss brought on by the crusade and not interested at all in the crusade itself, and woman as viewed by the crusader and imagined by him as a crusade supporter. He begins by blessing her ("Wol si, saelic wîp," 95,6) as a woman whose goodness can cause her to be taken over seas ("daz man si vüeret über sê," 95,8). This seems clearly to be a reference to the stowaway motif of the poem's second stanza, where the crusader declared himself ready to take Minne, worldly love, on his trip "in gotes lant" (94,33). The crusader will thus take Minne and his "saelic wîp" over seas, with Minne apparently serving as metaphorical stand-in. For he pictures the woman remaining at home, suffering in concern for him ("wande ir heime tuot alsô wê," 95,11), much like the "gente" beloved in Guiot's 'Chanterai por mon corage.' He also pictures her praying for him which, interestingly enough, the woman in Guiot's poem is portrayed as actually doing, but which in Johansdorf's Wechsel occurs only in the crusader's imagination. Here the attempt to bridge the tension between worldly love and crusade duty is a male undertaking encompassing the manner in which the woman is viewed by crusader. By contrast, in the portrayal of the woman in her own words, the crusades and its concerns, though confronting her also, are never mentioned or referred to explicitly. The man talks about the crusade and about his daydreams of her support for his crusade participation; the woman speaks only of the dire results of this participation for her quality of life. The viewpoints of crusader and beloved woman are totally at odds and apparently irreconcilable.

Otto von Botenlauben

In contrast to Johansdorf, Otto von Botenlauben's crusade *Wechsel 'Waere Kristes lôn niht alsô süeze'* (KLD 41,XII) features what appears at first to be harmony between male and female speech and viewpoint. In the first stanza of this *Wechsel*, as we heard previously, the crusader informs us that if it were not for "Kristes lôn," (1,1) he would not have left at home "al umbe den Rîn" (1,5) the good woman whom he calls his kingdom of heaven ("mîn himelrîche," 1,4). In the companion strophe, we now hear the woman respond directly to these words of adoration:

> 'Sît er giht ich sî sîn himelrîche,
> sô habe ich in zuo gote mir erkorn,
> daz er niemer fuoz von mir entwîche.
>   (KLD 41,XII, 2,1-3)

> [Since he calls me his kingdom of heaven,
> So I have chosen him as my god,
> So that he will never move a step from me.]

To his "bold metaphor" characterizing her as his kingdom of heaven, she thus responds with an at least equally bold designation of him as her chosen god. To this she adds the intriguing elaboration that, as her god, he is never to leave her. Thus apparently in response specifically to his statement that he would not leave her were it not for "Kristes lôn," she would expressly require that he not leave her at all. As in the poems of Johansdorf, the man's concession to crusade duty, though reluctant, is not shared by the woman or, in any case, not at first. She follows this tacit challenge to his crusade commitment with a prayer that begins and ends, not exactly in gestures of reconciliation, and certainly not of submission, but, in any case, with pleas to God for understanding:

> 'herr got, lâ dirz niht wesen zorn.
> erst mir in den ougen niht ein dorn,

der mir hie ze fröiden ist geborn.
kumt er mir niht wider, mîn spilnde fröide derst verlorn.'
(2,4-7)
[Lord God, do not let that anger you.
The one who was born for my joy
Is after all not a thorn in my eye.
If he does not come back my joy is gone.]

God is here called upon to see things from the woman's point of view
and to understand her fear of losing to the crusade the man whom she
pictures as her only source of joy. The woman portrayed in
Johansdorf's *Frauenstrophen* saw things very much the same way.
What is new here, however, is that Botenlauben has the woman express
this view in a prayer. Actually, in Botenlauben's *Wechsel*, both the man
and the woman pray, and indeed with a telling difference. The man
asks God for help to gain His favor for his beloved and himself; the
woman prays for God's understanding of her being concerned only
about the danger of losing her beloved man. As in the poetry of
Johansdorf, only the man concerns himself with service to God. The
woman focuses in both cases exclusively on her endangered
relationship—as in Botenlauben's *Wechsel*, where she makes this
relationship a matter of prayer, so also in Johansdorf's poem where she
does not.

Friedrich von Leiningen

As we heard above, the last stanza of Friedrich von
Leiningen's '*Swes muot ze fröiden sî gestalt*' (KLD 12), opens with a
woman's words of blessing for her crusader beloved who is about to
depart. In response to the crusader's request for this blessing in the
preceding stanza, she prays as follows:

'In guoter stunde sî dîn vart,
dîn lîp dîn sêle sî bewart,
dîn lop dîn heil dîn êre!
    (KLD 12,5,1-3)

[May your travel be in a propitious hour,
May your body and soul be preserved,
Along with your praise, salvation, and honor!]

Actually, uttering this prayer has required a considerable effort and indeed one which has been made in response to the crusader's request. He has asked her, namely, to temper her mood ("senfte ein kleine dînen muot," 4,7) and to lift his spirits ("hoehent miner fröiden hort," 4,10) by speaking just five words of blessing.

Her exercise in temperance does not last long. Her blessing is followed immediately by the following stern words of displeasure:

> 'mac dichs niht wenden mîn gebot
>   mîn flê mîn dröu, daz weiz wol got,
> sô wil ich biten sêre.
> Sît daz dîn vart unwendic ist,
> zwei herze in arebeite,
> daz mîn und dîn, du füerest hin
> dâ von ich iemer trûric bin:
> nu sî Krist dîn geleite!'
>   (5,4-11)

> [Since you cannot be deterred by my command,
> My pleading, my threatening--God knows—
> So I will ask you fervently.
> Since your travel is irreversible,
> So you will take with you two hearts in distress,
> Mine and yours,
> Which will leave me forever sad.
> Now may Christ be your guide!]

Clearly, the crusader is leaving for the crusade with her blessing, but against her express wishes. Furthermore, according to her own words, her resistance to his enlistment has been substantial and intense. And while her blessing did mention his salvation among her wishes for him, the focus of the blessing, like that of her counterpart in the poetry of Johansdorf and Botenlauben, is clearly the person of her beloved and nearly excludes his crusade venture. In fact, her blessing is quite obviously an interruption (extracted by his explicit request) in a strong expression of anti-crusade sentiment. He is departing over her very pointed objections.

Der Burggraf von Lienz

While the sixth and final strophe of the Burggraf von Lienz's 'Ez gienc ein juncfrou minneclîch' (KLD 36,I), transmitted in

Manuscript C, is clearly crusade poetry, the preceding five strophes are
not. These consist of a narrative *Serena*-cum-*alba* depicting the arrival
and departure of a knight who spends the night with a "juncfrou
minneclîch" (1,1) while a watchman, who greets him upon arrival,
stands guard. The parting words of the woman in stanza four contain a
blessing, but no reference to a crusade. Furthermore, the speaker in the
crusade strophe--it is not clearly certain that he is the knight of the
previous stanzas--says nothing about parting from an individual, but
instead refers only to his "friunde" (6,2; MHG = 'friends' or 'relatives')
and "die lieben" (6,8; MHG = 'the loved ones') in the plural. Thus it is
not expressly indicated that the woman's parting words of blessing
have anything to do with the crusade. On the other hand, since they
occur in a poetic complex in which a companion strophe is a crusade
stanza, it also cannot be ruled out that the woman is indeed blessing a
departing crusader. Comparison with the similar poem by Leiningen
speaks in favor of this view, and one could wonder if the similarity is
coincidental. Did one of these poets influence the other?

After rousing the knight at the prompting of the watchman, the
"juncfrou minneclîch" first commends herself to the knight, whom she
cherishes above all others. Then she tells him that she has his heart with
her and wants him to take hers with him. This is the traditional
exchange of hearts from which the woman in Leiningen's poem departs
by suggesting that the departing crusader should take both hearts. It is
here that Lienz's "juncfrou minneclîch" commends her furtive lover to
the highest God. However, her final words (and the closing words of
the poem) constitute an emphatic expression of displeasure at his
parting:

> 'du lâ mich dir bevolhen sîn
> als dû mir bist für alle man:
> bî mir hân ich daz herze dîn,
> des mînen ich dir vil wol gan.
> Dem hôhsten gote bevilhe ich dich.
> ein scheiden von dir riuwet mich.'
>   (KLD 36,I,4,5-10)

> [Let me be commended to you
> As you are to me above all men:
> I have your heart with me,
> And mine I gladly grant to you.
> I commend you to the Highest God.
> Parting from you grieves me.]

While the exchange-of-hearts motif is strikingly different, the portrayal of the woman in this stanza is otherwise very similar to that in Friedrich von Leiningen's '*Swes muot ze fröiden sî gestalt*' (KLD 12). Here as there the woman wants to send the crusader off with assurance of her lasting affection. In both she utters a blessing that includes no trace of the support for the crusader as crusader is called for (by a man) in Hartmann's '*Swelch vrowe sendet ir lieben man*' (MF 211,20) and imagined (by a man) in Johansdorf's '*Guote liute, holt die gâbe*' (MF 94,15). Instead, that blessing is addressed only to the man as beloved. And, finally, like her counterpart in the poems of Johansdorf, the woman as portrayed by Lienz, as by Leiningen, makes clear that her crusader is departing over her express objections and to her considerable annoyance.

Summary Of Part II. The Female Persona In Medieval German Crusade Poetry

Only a small number of medieval German crusade poems have been preserved which feature or include the portrayal of a woman. A few common features make them noteworthy. While all were composed by men and, in fact, by some of the same male poets whose poems we heard previously, women are portrayed differently from men in a consistent way. Only the man talks about the crusade, the woman does not. In this the German poems differ from the two Romance poems with which we compared them: the woman as portrayed in the poems of Marcabru and Guiot de Dijon does refer to the crusades in which her man is participating. In the portrayal of the woman in German poetry there is no such recognition. Instead, the woman objects to the crusader's departure and in some cases she confronts the crusader directly with these objections.

In the portrayal of the crusader, we heard the man struggle to cope with crusade duty as a problem fraught with considerable tension. The call to duty proved difficult to reconcile with strong attachment to the homeland including devotion to the beloved woman. In the portrayal of the woman in medieval German crusade poetry there is nothing to reconcile. For her there is only the threat of losing her beloved to the crusade as a rival, a rival which, in the German poems, she herself never specifically mentions. Clearly, then, our poets picture the woman's discomfort with the crusade as stronger than that of the crusader, opposing her firm and unwavering objection to his inner conflict and struggle. To be sure, the small number of examples requires that one generalize cautiously. Nevertheless, the consistency of this pattern seems to belie coincidence.

As noted previously, German crusade poetry as we know it began during the later twelfth century, that is, during an age in which anti-crusade sentiment was widespread in Europe. Germany's first poet of crusade songs, the historical crusader Friedrich von Hausen, probably composed his poems not long before departing on the crusade which cost him his life in 1190. In 1201 was published the decretal *Ex multa* of Pope Innocent III, in which the Pope stipulated for the first time that "men might freely make and fulfill the crusade vow...even should their wives not give their assent to the proposal."[140] This ruling reversed canonistic opinions, going back to the *Decretum* of Ivo of Chartres during the First Crusade, which had essentially given a wife veto power over her husband's crusade commitment. On the basis of a legal opinion expressed in his *Decretum,* Ivo had written to a nobleman that "(i)f his wife would not consent to his absence on the crusade, then he must abstain from joining the crusade in order to satisfy his wife's desire for his company."[141] Thus the poems we have heard, in which a woman objects in strong terms to the departure of a beloved crusader, were composed during a period in which such objections on the part of medieval European wives were about to be ruled null and void. Although the woman in our poems is never specifically identified as wife, one could still wonder if there might not be a connection between the portrayal in poetry of a woman objecting to a beloved man's participation in a crusade and the imminent overruling of a canonical opinion privileging her objections.

Of course, all of this must remain speculation. Still, one might well be tempted to see these poems as reflections of discussions and interest triggered by the impending change in regard to an issue of considerable importance for women. In coming to grips with the pressures of crusade obligation on a laity that still remembered the disasters of previous expeditions, our poets may quite conceivably have functioned as the public voices of a class, or classes, once again called upon to assume the burden of war against a formidable enemy. In any case, it is quite apparent that at least a few medieval poets took it upon themselves to provide articulation for the concerns of women who viewed themselves as crusade victims.

PART III.
The Crusade Observer Of Unknown Status

Introduction

In the crusade poems of several German poets there is no clear indication whether the speaker portrayed is to be seen as a crusader or as an interested non-fighter. These include some of the most interesting crusade poems in the German tradition. The poets in question are Heinrich von Rugge (attested 1175-1178?), Rubin (1st half of the 13th century), and Neidhart (c. 1185-c. 1240).

Each of these three poets presents a different perspective on the crusade and crusade participation. At the same time, one feature is common to all. The speaker in each case gives the impression of being a crusader without explicitly claiming to be one. Neidhart's crusade song, which is strongly anti-crusade, is set expressly in the war zone without indicating what the speaker is doing there. In the two crusade poems by Rugge, which are just as strongly pro-crusade, there is a good deal of talk about going to war but no clear indication that the speaker is going himself. The poems of Rubin are pro-crusade like those of Rugge, but encompass features which threaten to distract and perhaps even detract from their pro-crusade message.

Heinrich von Rugge

Members of a Rugge family were unfree knights, *ministeriales* (MHG *dienestman*), of the Count of Tübingen in Southwest Germany. A *"Heinricus miles de Rugge"* is attested once as witness to a document recorded in a monastery near Ehingen between 1175 and 1178.[142] It is not certain whether he is to be identified with the poet who authored the crusade poems that have been preserved under this name.

The Leich (MF 96,1; KD 32)

Heinrich von Rugge's *Leich*, transmitted in Manuscript N (Munich, clm 4570), is one of two poems by him which deal with the crusades. In the *Leich*, Rugge laments the death of Emperor Frederick Barbarossa (97,12ff) that took place in 1190, so that one can reasonably assume that the *Leich* was composed shortly afterward.

At the beginning of Rugge's *Leich* 'Ein tumber man' (MF 96,1; KD 32), the speaker identifies himself as an ignorant man dispensing wise advice ("wîsen rât," 96,2), wiser indeed than the dispenser himself (96,6f). This advice will bring great gain to listeners who heed it ("daz wirt iu ein vil grôz gewin," 96,5). His mouth, the mouth of an ignorant man, as he emphasizes again (96,9f), will make known the fashioning of God's wonders ("wiez um gotes wunder ist getân," 96,11). We then hear two aspects of God's wonders. First comes the concise warning (96,13-16) that whoever does not serve Him is doomed, for God's anger will befall him direly ("harte," 96,16). Then comes a (slightly longer) passage (96,17-24) in which are proffered in the wise words from the mouth of an ignorant man ("wîses mannes wort/von tumbes mannes munde," 96,17f), as the speaker reminds us again, the lasting rewards of heaven (96,19 and 24).

In the next section (96,25ff), the speaker brings himself into the picture. He begins by including himself in a group that needs to seek those heavenly rewards. He himself aspires to the same blessedness: "jâ teil ich mir/ die selben saelekeit" (96,25f). If he can serve appropriately ("dar nâch," 96,27), grace is "mir gereit" ('guaranteed'? 'available'? 'reserved'? to him). If he can leave off the silly lust ("verbir die bloeden gir," 97,2) in his heart, then he will be off to the (heavenly) joys of which he has heard such wondrous things.

In most of the poems of our first group, and in all of the longer ones, the speaker's status as a crusader is made unmistakably clear, notably through a reference to his having taken the cross or, in Hausen's case, to his commitment to fight the heathen. In Rugge's *Leich*, however, the speaker considers and outlines carefully the opportunities of crusading and exhorts his listeners to participate, but he does not indicate his own participation, whether current or intended.

The lament for Emperor Frederick is strikingly brief:

Nu sint uns starkiu maere komen:
diu habent ir alle wol vernommen.
Nu wünschent algelîche
heiles umbe den richen got--
wande er revulte sîn gebot
an keiser Friderîche...
(MF 97, 7-12)

Now we have received dire news
Which you have all heard.
Now let everyone wish for
Salvation from Mighty God--
For he fulfilled his command
In Emperor Frederick...

This wording, according to the punctuation of this passage in the standard editions, is curious, since it has God obeying His own command.[143] In any case, the Emperor and the many other pilgrims ('ander manege bilgerîn,' 97,15) are examples of those who have obtained the heavenly reward. Their situation is good ("vil schöne," 97,16), their souls are with God, who will never leave them. The speaker exhorts his hearers to follow their examples and take advantage of the same opportunity. He presents this opportunity metaphorically as a market place, a metaphor that was used in crusade sermons, but also in the Latin crusade poem 'Fides cum Ydolatria' (KL 6).[144] Whoever buys in time is blessed, he announces, for God gives wonderful tender ("marke," 97,22). And again he includes himself without actually indicating his own status:

> jâ vinden wir gereit
> lediclîchen âne strît
> grôz liep âne allez leit.
> Nu werbent nâch dem wunneclîcheme heile.
> (MF 97,23-23)

> [We will find freely
> Available without contention
> Great pleasure without sorrow.
> Let us strive for this wondrous salvation.]

At this point comes an apparent change of scene as well as topic. The speaker feels provoked to respond to the lamentation of people around him whom one ("man," 97,27) hears lamenting the loss of loved ones ("vriunde," 97,28), meaning, as he will clearly indicate, loved ones who have fallen on crusade. The speaker thus locates himself (at home) among the mourners. He objects to their lamentation and wants to introduce a different perspective ("ein ander maere sagen," 97,30). His words are:
iHi

> Swer si weinet, derst ein kint.
> daz wir niet sîn, dâ sî dâ sint,
> daz ist ein schade, den wir michels gerner möchten weinen.
> (MF 97,35-37)

> [Whoever mourns for them is a (silly) child.
> That we are not where they are,

That is a lack that we should much rather be mourning.]

Then comes a section of six lines in which the heavenly bliss of fallen crusaders is described in lush and emotional tones. Their situation is one of great honor ("nâch grôzen êren," 98,3) since they have received the heavenly crown without strife or envy ("sunder strît und âne nît," 98,5) and have been appointed an eternal and blissful reward (nâch wunneclîchem lône," 98,12).

This section, in turn, leads smoothly into a rousing call to enlistment in the crusades. Lines 98,13 thru 99,20 of Heinrich von Rugge's *Leich* set a standard for German crusade poetry as a recruitment elocution for which there is no known model in German poetry and which, to my knowledge, found no successor. The speaker begins with the curious assertion that the devil uttered the **same** scorn: "Der tiufel huob den selben spot" (98,13). What scorn is meant is not clear; the previous lines of the text, where there is no indication of a problem in transmission, extolled the bliss of heaven for the fallen crusader without any mention of scorn.[145] The speaker continues with a statement that seems strikingly original. Going back at least as far as the encyclica *Quantum praedecessores* of Pope Eugene III, Christian defeats in crusade warfare had been explained as having been caused by the sins of Christians on both sides of the Mediterranean ("nostris et ipsius populi peccatis exigentibus").[146] In Rugge's *Leich* the same idea is expressed, with characteristic folksiness, in the following quaint vignette:

> entslâfen was der rîche got
> dur daz wir brâchen sîn gebot.
> in hât sîn genâde erwecket.
> (MF 98,14-16)

> [The powerful God had fallen asleep
> Because we broke his commandment.
> Now his grace has awakened him.]

God, who had gone to sleep because of our disobedience, has been aroused by his mercy and has decided to wake up and help. God will now take care of us himself ("unser sêle pflegen," 98,18), but not alone, for he has a lot of fine warriors ("vil manigen stolzen degen," 98,19 = crusaders or angels?) at his disposal. The evil ones (= the Saracens? Satanic forces?) are terrified: "die boesen sint erschrecket" (98,21).

Having prepared for it very carefully, the speaker can now make his appeal, an appeal whose formulation is an intriguing mixture. On the one hand, it is worded to address the ethos of knights and certainly of the (fellow-?)knights whom he is trying to recruit:

Swer nü daz crûce nimet,
wie wol daz helden zimet!
daz kumt von mannes muote.
(MF 98,21-23)

[Whoever now takes the cross,
How fitting that is for heroes!
That stems from manly courage.]

On the other hand, the very next words depart abruptly from this tone of bravado and draw on the theme of assurance sounded in the section that led up to the appeal:

Got der guote in sîner huote
<si> ze allen zîten hât,
der niemer sî verlât.
(MF 98,21-27)

[The good God will
Keep them in his care at all times
And never leave them.]

Thus the speaker addresses his hearers with an interesting double message. On the one hand, he appeals to their manly courage; on the other he is at pains to reassure them of divine care. Apparently, he assumes that his heroes, with all their bravery, will still need to be assured of protection.

In the next lines we hear the speaker confront an opposing view, perhaps in an attempt to strengthen his words of reassurance. He imagines the words of a worthless man ("ein boeser man," 98,28) who contradicts his message by exhorting potential recruits rather to stay at home and pass the time pleasantly with women (98,30f). In response to this suggestion, our speaker imagines a woman who is the object of this detractor's desire ("der er dâ gert," 98,33) and has this imagined woman reply to him. She tells a girl friend ("gespile"), namely, that this kind of man would be a total waste of time:

> waz sol er danne ze vriuntschefte mir?
> Vil gerne ich in verbir.
> (MF 98,36f)

> [What kind of romance can he offer me?
> How gladly will I do without him.]

To this sentiment her girl friend agrees wholeheartedly (98,37b). Thus not only does our speaker have the crusade shirker condemned before God, he also has him condemned by women as a worthless suitor.

After adding a few words of his own in condemnation of crusade shirkers (99,38-99,2), our dispenser of wisdom returns again to his direct and fervent appeal for enlistment. This appeal continues to be formulated in such a way that the speaker's own position remains unclear. The follow passage is typical:

> Ich râte iu, dar ich selbe wil:
> nu nement daz crûce und varent dâhin,
> daz wirt iu ein vil grôze gewin,
> unde vürhtent niht den tôt.
>   (MF 99,17-20)

> [I advise you to go where I want to go:
> Take the cross and go there.
> It will be great gain for you.
> And do not be afraid of death.]

These words of one who wants to go on crusade give the impression that he is not going. He does not invite others to join him, but rather urges them onto a path that, to all appearances, he himself (cannot or) will not take.

In the closing section of the poem, the speaker returns to his pose as an ignorant man dispensing wise advice and identifies himself by name as "Der tumbe man von Rugge" (99,21). If the poet is indeed the historical "Heinricus miles de Rugge"—which is impossible to verify—then perhaps we are to view him as an aged man unable to go on a crusade in which he fervently believes and in which he would like to take part. Wisdom was, after all, commonly associated with the elderly in the Middle Ages.[147] The dates of the historical Rugge might fit such an interpretation very well since he may have been advanced in years by the time of the Third Crusade of Barbarossa who, one should note however, was at that time advanced in years himself.

In any case, the unwavering espousal of the crusades in Rugge's *Leich* sets this speaker apart from all of the voices heard in the works of lay poets encountered in this study up to now. The piety expressed in this *Leich* is unequivocal. On the other hand, the speaker in this poem equivocates in another way by leaving unclear throughout this lengthy poem whether he is himself a crusader. This sets him apart from the lay poets discussed whose poems clearly portray a man enlisted in the crusades.

'Ich was vil ungewon' (MF 102,1; KD 33)

In this poem of two strophes by Heinrich von Rugge, transmitted in Manuscript C, only the second stanza (MF 102,14) contains what seems to be a clear reference to a crusade.[148] The opening announcement of this crusade strophe is very much in the spirit of the *Leich*:

Des liebes[149] habe ich mich dur got vil gar bewegen,
ez waer ein tumber wân, dûhte ich mich des ze guot.
(MF 102,14-17)

[I have taken leave of pleasure for God's sake,
It would be vainglory to vaunt myself about this.]

These words sound like the pronouncement of a new crusader. However, strictly speaking, the speaker only says that he has made a decision for God and against that which is pleasurable. Thus, as in the *Leich*, he seems to identify himself as a crusader, but in point of fact it is not certain that he does so.[150]

He continues by pointing out that God let himself be wounded caring for us, so that repaying him would be a blessed act ("wie saeliclîch er tuot!" 102,21). Similarly in the *Leich* proud heroes ("stolze helde," 99,3) were avised that he is blessed ("saelic," 99,4) who can die in the same place where God died. We are foolish to rage about possessions, he continues (102,22), adding that for the sake of a better reward ("bezzer lôn," 102,26) he would quickly surrender a thousand lands, retaining only seven feet (= his grave) for himself.

Although the crusade is not mentioned expressly, here speaks without doubt an unreserved crusade enthusiast. The strophe is therefore very much of a piece with Rugge's *Leich*. Like the latter, it stops short of the clear identification of the speaker as a crusader, but shares the *Leich*'s clear expression of crusade enthusiasm.

This enthusiasm contrasts sharply with the ardent complaining which dominates the portrayal of the crusader in the poems of Rugge's fellow German poets of the twelfth century. There is no place in Rugge's poetry for remonstrating with God about making women so beautiful that they distract the crusader from proper commitment, for moans of distress about having to leave the homeland to fulfill an obligation which interrupts a joyful life, nor for leering (enviously?) at those who have evaded crusade duty and intend to benefit from their cowardice. The enthusiasm expressed for the crusades in the poems of Heinrich von Rugge serves to set by contrast in vivid relief the ardent complaints and equivocal piety in the poems of his fellow-poets.

This crusade strophe from '*Ich was vil ungewon*' follows in Manuscript C a strophe in the same metrical form (MF 102,1) where we hear the complaints of a man facing an unaccustomed situation. He has been freed from the cares of love, having been dismissed by the discomfiting greeting ("ein ungemacher gruoz," 102,6) of a woman ("wîp," 102,13) who once indicated that his soul and body were as dear to her as hers to him. Now she has changed completely ("gar verkêrt," 102,13) her attitude toward him. There is nothing in this stanza which connects it clearly with the crusade or, for that matter, with the crusade stanza '*Des lîbes habe ich mich dur got vil gar bewegen*' (MF 102,14). I am enclined, with hesitation, to agreement with Hölzle[151] in seeing the two strophes as independent compositions in the same meter. My hesitation has a general and a specific reason. The general reason is that we have already encountered in our study a number of cases where the pangs of love, and usually of unrequited love, are somehow linked expressly with crusade commitment. The specific reason is that we shall encounter a juxtaposition of unhappy love and crusade enlistment very similar to the one in these stanzas of Rugge when we discuss below the poet Rubin to whom Rugge's poetry seems to have been well known.

Neidhart

Neidhart was an extraordinarily popular and very original poet[152] about whom almost nothing is known. After decades of scholarship his birthplace remains unknown, his home and field of activity can be delimited only vaguely as the Bavarian-Austrian area, and neither his name form nor its status (real name or artistic pseudonym?) can be determined.[153]

There are also important uncertainties about his crusade poetry. Of the two Neidhart-poems which Müller includes in his crusade anthology, '*Ez gruonet wol diu heide*' (KD 69 = SL 11) and '*Komen sint uns die liehten tage lange*' (KD 70 = SL 12[154]), Müller himself raises doubts elsewhere whether the second of these poems is actually a crusade song at all.[155] And, in point of fact, the speaker in '*Komen sint uns die liehten tage lange*' reports only that he belongs to an unidentified group of returning travelers who are now approaching the Rhine ("wir nâhen zuo dem Rîne," SL 12,V,3). Like '*Ez gruonet wol diu heide*,' the poem '*Komen sint uns die liehten tage lange*' also includes the sending of a messenger with greetings to the homeland and the singling out of a beloved woman ("dem liepgenaemen wîbe, SL 12,VII,1), this time for a special greeting to her alone. However, there is in '*Komen sint uns die liehten tage lange*' no indication that the travel in the poem is a crusade, and indeed the fact that the travelers are approaching the Rhine on the return trip would seem to indicate otherwise. Thus despite similarities with '*Ez gruonet wol diu heide*' which might suggest a crusade connection, it will not be included in our discussion. '*Ez gruonet wol diu heide*' is the only poem by Neidhart that is clearly and explicitly linked with a crusade.

This poem begins with a nature introduction, *Natureingang*, a traditional stylistic device which Neidhart used in very original ways.[156] In '*Ez gruonet wol diu heide*,' the *Natureingang* of two stanzas describes the winter's violent subjection of the summery heath and forest: "der winder kalt/ twanc si sêre beide" (SL 11, I, 3f). It occurs to the speaker that, while he is hearing the singing birds in this change of seasons, they are also being heard by his loved ones ("den vriunden mîn") far away. He wishes for an opportunity to sing for the latter a song which would garner their acclaim ("des sî mir alle sagten danc," II,5). As matters stand, however, his own singing is poorly received: the "Walhen" (the French? the Italians? both?)[157] pay no attention to his singing (II,6f), a distressing thought which provokes a sigh of blessing on the German language: "sô wol dir, diutschiu zunge!" (II,7)

The speaker here is thus far from home among foreign companions. The poem has usually been thought to reflect events and situations in Damietta, Egypt during the crusade of 1217-1221.[158] In any case, the speaker locates himself in the war arena like the crusader in Reinmar's 'Des tages dô ich daz kriuze nam' (MF 181,13) discussed above. Both poets also have their speaker entrust greetings for loved ones (vriunde) in the homeland to a messenger or messengers (Reinmar MF 181,37; Neidhart SL 11, IV, 1f). In Reinmar's case, the messengers are the speaker's wayward thoughts, gedanke, which beset him with longing for the old life. In Neidhart's poem, the messenger seems to be, similarly, a creation of the speaker's imagination: first we hear him say how gladly he would like to send home a messenger familiar with his village ("der daz dorf erkande," III, 4) where he left a lovelorn woman ("die seneden," III, 5); a few lines later, we hear him addressing a messenger and commanding him to depart with greetings for his "lieben vriunden" over seas (IV, 1f). Then, however, after we have heard the contents of his message (four stanzas worth), we immediately hear him announce that, if the messenger delays ("sûme," VIII, 1), he will be his own messenger: "sô wil ich selbe bote sîn" (VIII, 2). In Neidhart's case also, then, we seem to be dealing with an imaginary, metaphorical messenger used to express the intensity of longing for a beloved homeland and beloved vriunde.

It is only in Neidhart's poem, however, not in Reinmar's, that we hear the specifics of the message. Here the speaker instructs the messenger to take a message from a group ("von uns," IV,5) to the "vriunden" and to tell them that only the width of the ocean ("des wâges breite," IV,7) keeps them from being reunited at home. The speaker continues his instructions by committing to the messenger a special homage to his "meisterinne" (wife?)[159] whom he promises to love from now on above all ladies ("vür all vrouwen hinne vür," V,5). To the "vriunden unde magen" ('friends and relatives') the messenger is to give a report which sounds a little contradictory: First the messenger is to say that he is doing well ("daz ich mich wol gehabe," VI,2); but if they question him further, then the messenger is to report the following:

> sô sage, wie wê
> uns die Walhen haben getân. des muoz uns hie betrâgen.
> (SL 11,VI, 6f)

> [So tell them how much pain
> The Walhen have caused us. That has to vex us deeply.]

The messenger is then hurried off with the promise that the speaker will follow as soon as he can ("so ich aller baldist immer mac," VII,5). No sooner has the messenger departed, however, when we hear the speaker pondering the possibility of being his own messenger and reporting the whole truth of the situation:

> wir leben alle kûme,
> das her ist mêr dan halbez mort.
> (SL 11,VIII,4f)
> [We are all scarcely alive,
> More than half the army is dead.]

Thus while in Reinmar der Alte's similar poem, *'Des tages dô ich daz kriuze nam'* (MF 181,13), bitter aversion to crusading was conveyed with subtlety and indirectness, at least at the beginning, here it is spelled out with unabashed explicitness. Neidhart's references to the condition of the army and to suffering at the hands of the "Walhen" have no counterpart in Reinmar's poem where we heard the crusader refer to his surroundings only in his revelation that he is not the only one suffering "sorge" with his thoughts ("si tuot ouch mêre liuten wê," MF 181,22). And the somewhat detailed instructions to the messenger in Neidhart's poem had as meager counterpart in Reinmar's only the request to the *gedanke* that they greet common friends ("unser beider vriunde dort gegrüezen," MF 181,37) during their furlough in the homeland. The crusader in Reinmar's poem also adds fond thoughts of home back-handedly in his curious words of blessing to *vröide*: he simultaneously remembers this personified "joy" as an overnight companion while claiming to have forgotten the same episode (MF 182,7f). By contrast, in Neidhart's poem this longing is formulated explicitly in the speaker's desire to be lying in his space beside the fair one: "bî der wolgetânen laege ich gerne an mînem rûme" (SL 11,VIII, 7). Finally, while aversion to the crusade in Reinmar's poem was expressed subtly in the crusader's shocking offer of servile submission to anyone who would extract him from his present distress and put him back on the road to the blessed *vröide* of yore (MF 182,13f), in Neidhart's poem the same aversion is expressed barshly in the speaker's pronouncement that anyone who remains in the war zone until August is a fool (SL 11,XI, 1f).

Since the directness and explicitness of Neidhart's *"Ez gruonet wol diu heide'* contrasts in all these respects with the indirectness and subtlety of Reinmar's *'Des tages dô ich daz kriuze nam,'* it is all the more noteworthy that only the poem by Reinmar makes clear that the speaker is a crusader. The poems of both show distaste for the crusade and the desire to be at home. It is Neidhart, however, who provides the kind of suggestive details that have stimulated proposals about dating, location, and even about personal involvement of Neidhart in one or more specific crusades.[160] The impression given by Reinmar is a vague one that the crusader is somewhere in the war zone with people who suffer the same distress as he. No suggestive detail or suggestion of detail breaks through the vaguery of that impression.

On the other hand, Reinmar portrays a crusader who clearly identifies himself as such. By contrast, Neidhart does not. Actually, in his poem, the speaker presents himself as a performer whose poor reception by the "Walchen" causes him to bless the German language. Like Rugge, though unlike him in his anti-crusade stance, Neidhart portrays a speaker who talks of a crusading army whose difficulties he shares without indicating that he himself is a soldier in that army.

Rubin

We know nothing factual about the life of the poet Rubin. Kornrumpf considers it certain ("mit Sicherheit") that Rubin was active before the death of Walther von der Vogelweide around 1230.[161] Von Kraus characterizes Rubin as probably a minstrel who ventured into the sphere of high courtly love.[162]

Rubin's 'Got hât uns aber sîn gemant' (KLD 47, VII A), transmitted in Manuscripts A and C, is a strongly worded call to crusading. It opens with a message from God reminding the listener that the sepulchre in which God lay and the land in which He suffered sacrificial death are both still in distress ("noch allez in der nôt," 1,2). At this thought the speaker crys out in horror that "we" care so little about that situation ("daz uns daz ie sô geringe wac!" 1,6). These words constitute a blanket indictment apparently designed to move qualified hearers to crusade enlistment. They also create an ambiguity: is this "we" purely rhetorical or does it include the speaker as himself a (potential) enlistee?

The second stanza opens with a warning to those who fail to heed the call:

Swer nû daz kriuze niht ennimt
der lîbes unde guotes hât
in vollen, daz ist missetân,
sô wol als ez der werlte zimt,

und ouch der sêle wirdet rât:
niht anders Ich gelouben hân.
(VII A,2,1-6)

[Whoever does not take the cross
Having bodily well being and possessions
In abundance, does wrong,
Since doing so would please the world
And provide for the soul:
I cannot see it any other way.]

In Walther von der Vogelweide's *'Owê waz êren sich ellendet tiuschen landen'* (L 13,5), one hears a challenge to those who have "witze unde manheit, dar zuo silber und daz golt" (13,6) that staying at home will mean disgrace, and that all who do so will forfeit the reward of the heavenly King ("des himeleschen keisers solt," 13,8). So also here in the quoted passage from Rubin's *'Got hât uns aber sîn gemant,'* hearers are warned that if one has good health and wealth, one is obligated to enlist in the crusade. The stanza ends with a prayer to God (of one line) that He may hear "our" poor cry of weakness ("die broede lâ dir, got, an uns vil armen sîn gekleit," 2,11).

The third and last stanza is a rather jolting departure from the preceding[163]--one is reminded of the jarring juxtaposition of crusade theme and *minne*-theme in the controversial case of Rugge's *'Ich was vil ungewon'* (MF 102,1) mentioned earlier. The speaker here is suddenly complaining in similar terms about how the mistreatment ("missebieten," VII A,3,1) of his beloved has caused him so much distress ("senelîchen muot," 3,2) that he has become despised by the world. Meanwhile, she has enjoyed his heaviness of heart ("swaere," 3,4). In so doing, she seems to have done him a spiritual favor. For her mistreatment of him apparently made him think about the blessed everlasting reward ("dem lone/ der süezen êwe staetekeit," 3,8) and wonder if bodily striving ("des lîbes arebeit," 3,10) could ever earn the heavenly crown from Him who wears the crown of crowns (3,11). Failure in earthly love seems to have turned his thought to godly gain.

Rubin's second crusade song, *'Ich wil urloup von friunden nemen'* (KLD 47,XXII; KD 68) is transmitted in three manuscripts. C has all five strophes, A the first three, and B the first strophe only.

Almost every line of Rubin's *'Ich wil urloub von friunden nemen'* calls to mind a passage from poems of Rubin's (older) fellow-poets. The opening line of the poem (according to manuscripts and standard edition), in which the speaker takes leave of his "friunden," reminds one of the parting from the "herren unde mâge" in Hartmann von Aue's *'Ich var mit iuwern hulden'* (MF 218,5) discussed earlier in this study. The second line, in which the speaker emphasizes that he is parting in body but not in heart ("dem lîbe und aber dem herzen niht," XXII, 1,2), calls to mind the situation in Friedrich von Hausen's *'Mîn herze und mîn lîp diu wellent scheiden'* (MF 47,9) where it is likewise the body that is willing to depart and the heart that wants to stay at home. The third and fourth lines, in which the speaker declares that the joy ("fröide," XXII,1,3) of his "friunden" will suit him ("gezemen," 1,3) and their pleasure delight him ("ich minne daz in liep geschiht," 1,4) is strikingly similar to the passage in Hiltbolt von Schwangau's *'Ez ist ein reht daz ich lâze den muot'* (KLD 24,XVII; KD 42) where the departing crusader bestows his share of "minne" on his "lieben friunden" (XVII,3,1) and wishes for them all that he would wish for himself ("haete ich ich iht liebers, daz, solte iuwer sîn," 3,4). Lines XXII,1,5-8 in Rubin's poem, where the speaker expresses the hope that he will be recompensed for the discomfort ("rehte unsanfte," 1,6) of parting from loved ones ("friundes scheiden," 1,6) by the happiness of finding them well off ("âne swaeren muot," 1,5) upon his return, seems to echo Friedrich von Hausen's *'Mîn herze den gelouben hât,'* lines 48,7-12 where the crusader laments in similar tones the pain of parting, and commits to God's providence those whom he leaves for His sake.

The second stanza of Rubin's *'Ich wil urloup von friunden nemen'* reminds one of Walther von der Vogelweide. As in Walther's *'Owe war sint verswunden'* (L 124, 1) the joy of the world to come is lost to those who pursue the joy of the present (124,33), so in Rubin's case he is conquered by cares ("sorgen," XXII,2,4) who deserts God for this world (2,1). As in Walther's poem such a decision is all the more foolish since the present world has become so dreary (124,18-23) so that even the birds are saddened by so much lamentation, so here in Rubin's poem good things are going down hill in such a fashion that the birds no longer sing as sweetly as usual (XXII,2,7).

In Rubin's stanza 3, the speaker concedes as one "fault" ("schulde," 3,1) of his that he likes some people better than others ("mir geviel ie under zwein der eine muotes baz," 3,6), and expresses the hope that, if this is a sin ("sol daz ein sünde sîn," 3,7), he can be forgiven by the One who created such differences in people ("als ungelîchez leben," 3,8). This "fault" of being discriminating with one's affection seems to echo stanza 3 of Reinmar's *'Ich was vrô,'*(MF

168,30), where the speaker serves notice that he can get along without those who can get along without him, and will never like those who do not care for him. Alternatively, the passage could be influenced by Walther von der Vogelweide's *'Vil wol gelobter got'* (L 26,3), where the speaker expresses similarly a strong preference for ("iemer lieber sîn," 26,11) those who treat one well, and prays to God for forgiveness otherwise ("vergib mir anders mîne schulde, 26,12).

In stanza 4 of Rubin's *'Ich wil urloup von friunden nemen,'* the speaker laments having to part quickly without taking leave properly from the beloved ("wer sagt ir danne mînen gruoz?" 4,3). Similarly the speaker in the last stanza of the Burggraf von Lienz's *'Ez gienc ein juncfrou minneclîch'* (KLD 36,I,6; KD 66,VI) also laments his departure without having said goodbye to loved ones ("der friunde," 6,2; "die lieben," 6,8), but here without singling out a beloved woman.

Both of Rubin's poems draw heavily on the works of his predecessors in the poetic tradition, not only in their details, but also in their totality. The first two strophes of his *'Got hât uns aber sîn gemant'* present a fervent call to crusading that reminds one of Heinrich von Rugge. The poem continues with a confession of a mistreated lover who turns to God on the rebound, a development familiar from the fourth strophe of Hausen's *'Sî darf mich des zîhen niet'* (MF 46,29-38). And Rubin's *'Ich wil urloup von friunden nemen'* we found to be, from beginning to end, a string of echoes from other poems. Rubin's crusade poetry thus gives the impression of being, in a very essential way, a literary exercise.

Here a further distinction needs to be made. We noted above that the poems which feature the portrayal of the crusader convey little of the lived experience implied by this portrayal, but focus mainly on the crusader's inner self as presented in a few repeatedly used stock situations. The repeated use of these situations is itself literary. For example, the portrayal of the crusader besieged by his wayward thoughts in Reinmar's *'Des tages dô ich daz kriuze nam'* (MF 181,13) is so similar to that of the crusader besieged by his wayward heart in Hausen's *'Mîn herze und mîn lîp diu wellen scheiden'* (MF 47,9) that coincidence is hardly conceivable. And since neither poem betrays much of the crusade experience, literary influence becomes all the more compelling as an explanation. A literary motif has been passed on, taken over, and modified. Despite Reinmar's very similar use of the motif, however, his portrayal of the crusader is a totally new one and presents a quite different fictional view of a crusade experience from that of Hausen. The two poems give us two rather distinct renditions of the mental/emotional state and thought processes of a crusader torn between duty and inclination.

By contrast, while Rubin's *'Got hât uns aber sîn gemant'* (KLD 47, VII A) presents us with a doctrinally impressive and unsettling crusade sermon, worthy of Rugge, followed by a confession of an unhappy love experience that has turned him to thoughts of God, it does not clearly present us with a crusader. Neither does his *'Ich wil urloup von friunden nemen'* (KLD 47, XXII). A few of its lines seem to give the impression that the speaker has indeed enlisted in a crusade: in the closing *Frauenstrophe*, the woman expresses the hope that her beloved will gain God's salvation for both ("uns erwerbe beiden gotes heil," 5,6). However, this literary reference to the man-woman crusade teamwork called for in poems of Hartmann and Johansdorf does not round out a clearly drawn portrayal of a crusader. Instead, it is, as noted, only one of a number of literary references which work against the kind of unified portrayal of the crusader that we know from the poetry of Hausen and Reinmar. Beginning and ending with a probable echo of Hartmann's poetry, Rubin's *'Ich wil urloup von friunden nemen'* is throughout a very literary poem. That is, it assembles an eclectic sampling of traditional literary motifs without achieving a cogent portrayal.

Summary of Part III. The Crusade Observer of Unknown Status

The poets Heinrich von Rugge, Neidhart, and Rubin all composed poems in which a speaker relates his views on crusading without betraying clearly whether he is himself a crusader. Heinrich von Rugge has a "dumb" man speaking wisdom conjure up an impressive array of figures and voices--including a recently awakened God, a scornful devil, and a staunchly sensible woman pursued by a worthless non-crusader--in support of an extended and passionate call to enlistment. Neidhart uses a typical opening of his summer song of love and the traditional figure of the messenger in a poem expressing bitter disgust at a crusade experience in which the horrible suffering of war is aggravated by conflict between European allies. Rubin's poems, like Rugge's, are strongly pro-crusade; but the passages complaining about unrequited worldly love, the distracting allusions to texts of his older fellow-poets, and the general tone of detachment in his poems give them the flavor of rote literary exercises.[164]

The speakers in the poems of all three poets betray, each in his own way, intense interest in the crusade. However, in contrast to the portrayal of the crusader in the poems of Hausen, Hartmann, Reinmar, Johansdorf, Botenlauben, Leiningen, and Lienz, the speaker in the poems of Rugge, Neidhart, and Rubin does not explicitly claim to be a soldier wearing the cross. Rugge presents the view of one who is passionately interested in the enthusiastic enlistment of others for a crusading expedition which will not clearly include his own participation. Neidhart presents the view from the actual arena of battle but without identifying the speaker as a (fellow)soldier in a beleagured army. And Rubin presents a mixture in which the crusades share the focus with worldly *minne* and literary allusions that gives one the sense that the crusade as an issue no longer has the immediacy that it once did. The crusades merely constitute one literary motif among many.

General Summary And Conclusion

Responses to the crusades in the poetry of medieval Europe varied widely. These poetic responses could also change over time as the example of medieval Latin crusade poetry clearly indicates. The Battle of Hattin had a profound impact on poetic expression in that tradition. The poetry of glib confidence in European superiority coupled, in a few cases, with graphic depictions of havoc wrought upon the enemy (including non-fighting bystanders) is replaced, after the defeat of the Christian forces in 1187, with a poetry which deemphasized the crusade as military undertaking per se, while touting it as an occasion for penitence and spiritual renewal.

Coeval with the Latin crusade poetry after Hattin are the crusade songs in the medieval German vernacular. The poetry of the Latin clerical sphere, from which issued the authoritative ideological declarations and instructions on crusading, coexists side by side with a parallel development in the poetry of the German laity whom these Latin ideological discourses targeted as the primary source of military personnel for crusade warfare.

The Latin crusade poetry after Hattin--that is, those poem that are contemporary with crusade poetry in the German vernacular--focus on God and on the crusades as an occasion for penitence and inner change. While this focus is not absent from the contemporary German crusade poems, it is quite rare and is generally relegated to the margins or is, in any case, far outweighed in significance by other concerns. Much more prominent, particularly in the German poems portraying the crusader, is the expression of a profound attachment to the homeland.

The crusade poems of Friedrich von Hausen, for instance, feature the powerful hold of the love for woman and home over the new crusader's heart. Some passages in his poems suggest that God should accept, others that He should even support this devotion of the heart to earthly love. In one of Hausen's poems, God is made responsible for the womanly beauty that distracts the man from crusade service. In another, service to God is made the measure of the man's worthiness of woman's affection: no self-respecting woman should love a man who shrinks back from crusade participation. In still another, God is called upon to see to it that the heart threatening to desert the crusader receives a good reception when it arrives at its destination. Otherwise, the crusader in these poems shows little interest in God and in penitence even less.

Johansdorf, Reinmar, and Botenlauben, whose poetry shows traces of Hausen's influence, vary his pattern only modestly. The crusader in Johansdorf's poems acknowledges openly the validity of the call to crusade service, but also makes known his firm devotion and commitment to his beloved and to *minne*. In Reinmar's crusade poems, a strong sense of obligation to crusading as a binding obligation is undermined and ultimately overthrown by the crusader's commitment to the worldly joy that the crusade has interrupted. Of course, in Reinmar's poetry as in Hausen's, the problem is aggravated by the crusader's insistence in both cases on siding with that part of his person—Hausen's *herze* like Reinmar's *gedanke*—which wants to forego crusade duty. In both cases obligation is pitted against inclination, and in Reinmar's *'Des tages dô ich daz kriuze nam'* (MF 181,13) it is clearly inclination that wins out.

Otto von Botenlauben's *'Waere Kristes lôn niht also süeze'* (KLD 41,XII) apparently attempts to reconcile obligation and inclination by offering God service partly on behalf of the beloved woman, his personal kingdom of heaven ("himelrîche'), whom he would expressly prefer not to leave for God's service. Similarly, in Hiltbolt von Schwangau's *'Ez ist ein reht'* (KLD 24,XVII; KD 42) the crusader prays to God to grant him, presumably upon his return, no other woman than the one whom he has left for His sake ("durch den ich sie lie"). Friedrich von Leiningen and Der Burggraf von Lienz resolve the tension somewhat differently by having the crusader focus on the crusade while using a female persona to express objection to the crusader's departure.

Hartmann von Aue alone departs from the pattern by seeming to reject the world and the practices of the minnesingers, though not woman or love per se. In his *'Swelch vrowe sendet ir lieben man'* (MF 211,20) the woman is assigned the role of seeing to it that her beloved crusader departs in the right frame of mind ("mit rehtem muote") and of remaining faithful to him and praying for him in his absence. Otherwise, Hartmann's poetry is addressed to men, specifically knightly men, who are exhorted to show their mettle by their loyalty to the cause of God. In turn, God is called upon for rescue from the dangerous ("vârende") hold of a beguiling Lady World, and to help the crusader gain entrance into tenth angelic choir ("den zehend kôr") replacing the devil. In Hartmann's poems, crusade commitment seems on the surface to have won out over worldly enticement, when in fact, on closer observation, the signs of a continuing struggle are all too evident.

The crusade poems portraying a woman (*Frauenlieder und Frauenstrophen*) feature complaints against the crusades from the woman's perspective. Consistently, the woman is portrayed as opposing the crusades with great intensity. This is not only true for German literature. Without exception, to my knowledge, in medieval Occitan and Old French poetry, as in the Middle High German, woman opposes crusade with a forcefulness not found in the poetry of men. While the voice of the man in a few German poems elicits female support for crusades and crusader, the voice of the woman addresses displeasure and even outrage about the crusade, be it to God (Marcabru, Guiot de Dijon), to at least one royal leader of a crusade (Marcabru), or to the crusader himself (Johansdorf, Leiningen, Lienz).

The poems of Heinrich von Rugge, Neidhart, and Rubin constitute a different case. In the crusade poems of all three we heard portrayals of a man who gives the impression of being a crusade participant without indicating explicitly that he is. While Rugge's poems are outspokenly pro-crusade and orthodox, those of Neidhart are equally outspoken in rejecting and even deriding crusade participation, whereas the poems of Rubin are noticeably detached in tone and marked by dependence on the literary past.

All German crusade poetry differs from Latin crusade poems composed after the Battle of Hattin in one respect. While the Latin poetry of this period formulates the call to crusading as a call to repentance and spiritual renewal, the German poems appeal to knightly prowess. We heard this expressed with particular emphasis in the poetry of Hartmann von Aue, for instance, in his challenge to knights whose shield has ever been ready to seek the high praise of the world ("zer welte bereit ûf hôhen prîs" (MF 210,3f). Similarly, the crusade sermon in Rubin's '*Got hât uns aber sîn ermant*' is addressed to the one who has fullness of bodily strength and of wealth ("der lîbes und guotes hât in vollen"). And Rugge's call to crusading is likewise a summons to an activity suitable for heroes ("wie wol daz helden zimet!" MF 98,22; "stolze helde," 99,3).

Latin crusade poetry after Hattin addresses the call to crusading in very different terms, exhorting men and women to pour out their hearts in penitence (*'Heu, voce flebili,'* KL 11), and calling on young men to turn their minds to the hereafter (*'Tonat evangelica,'* KL 23) and to sacrifice the love of "sanguinis et cognationum."

Medieval German crusade poetry, including the poems of Rugge, Neidhart, and Rubin, also departs from its Latin counterpart in devoting little attention to the actual warfare going on in the Holy Land, and particularly little to the "pagan" enemy. Latin poetry is explicit in identifying groups of enemies, usually by proper names, whether calling for or exulting in their defeat and annihilation, as in the earlier poems, or reacting to enemy successes and threats, as in the poems after Hattin. The German poems, by contrast, rarely mention this enemy, or even allied groupings, for that matter. The isolated references of Hartmann von Aue to "her Salatîn und al sîn her" (MF 218,19) and of Neidhart to "die Walchen" (SL 11,II,7) are exceptions which prove the rule.

Nowhere in medieval German crusade poetry is there anything comparable to the name lists (of allies and enemies) found in the Latin poems *'In toto mundo'* (KL 4) and *'Heu, voce flebili'* (KL 11). Walther von der Vogelweide's *'Der anagenge nie gewan'* (L 78,24; KD 52) does attack the angels Michael, Gabriel, and Raphael for their lack of effectiveness in destroying the heathen ("waz habet ir der heiden noch zerstoeret?" (79,3). However, even in his crusade poems, which offer an entirely different view of the crusades from the poems of our study, one finds no actual depictions of warfare and very little about the enemy. What one does find is a striking evenhandedness in Walther's references to the combatants in the Holy Land: Walther's *'Rich, here, dich und dine muoter'* (L 10,9; KD 55) calls on God let the Christians be wind to Him just like the heathens ("lâ dir den Kristen zuo den heiden sîn also den wint," (L 10,11); meanwhile, his *'Nû alrêst lebe ich mir werde'* (L 14,38; KD 59) caps a strikingly balanced depiction of the three-way conflict in Palestine by pronouncing the rightness of the Christian cause in a manner that suggests that this rightness is not self-evident. Thus Walther is an additional example of the restraint in medieval German crusade poetry's treatment of the enemy.

We have noted that God appears in both Latin and German crusade poetry in a variety of roles. Among the Latin poems composed after the Battle of Hattin, God appears in *'Plange, Sion'* (KL 12) and *'Jerusalem, luge'* (KL 14) as an angry deity punishing Christian sins by Christian defeat; in *'Crucifigat omnes'* (KL 13) as a suffering God crucified for the second time by defeat of the Christian cause through Christian sin; in *'Indue cilicium'* (KL 15) and *'Diro satis percussus vulnere'* (KL 25) as a puzzling and perplexing deity whose tolerance of Christian defeat and "pagan" insolence provokes incomprehension and consternation; in *'Tonat evangelica'* as a (liege) lord admonishing his subordinates concerning fealty owed; in *'Venit Jesus in propria'* (KL 17) as a beleaguered and solitary purveyor of the devastation and foreign occupation of His earthly homeland; in *'Quomodo cantabimus'* (KL 18) and *'Graves nobis admodum'* (KL 19) as the future avenger of present depradation; and, finally, in *'Miror, cur tepeat'* (KL 20) and *'Sede, Sion, in pulvere'* (KL 22) God is both the all-powerful Judge fully capable of vengeance against the enemy and the Purveyor of the human heart awaiting Christian repentance and spiritual renewal.

In German poetry, we encounter God in likewise varied but, for the most part, quite different roles. In the crusade poems of Heinrich von Rugge, we heard about God, apart from His awakening from sleep, mainly as the (proposed) beneficiary of knightly prowess. Neidhart's crusade poems mention God only once in a sigh of prayer for survival (SL 11,VII,7). The opening strophe of Rubin's *'Got hât uns aber sîn ermant'* echoes the opening of Johansdorf's *'Die hinnen varn'* (MF 89,21) in conveying the message to prospective crusaders that God's land is in trouble, a motif which we heard briefly in the Latin poem *'Quomodo cantabimus'* (KL 17). Rubin's poetry refers to God twice: in a prayer for "us" who strive for the wrong things" ("der sêle ein arebeit," KLD 47, VII A, 2,8) and in a confession that the speaker is not able to love people without showing preference ("mir geviel ie under zwein der eine muote baz," XXII,3,6). In Friedrich von Hausen's *'Sî darf mich des zîhen niht'* (MF 45,37), we heard the crusader make God responsible for having created the crusader's beloved so beautiful that his emotional attachment to her detracts from his dedication to the Holy Cause (MF 46,14-18 and 46,39-47,6). We heard the same crusader declare that he is now ready to serve the God who knows how to reward ("der lônen kan," 46,38) and regret that he has forgotten Him for so long (47,5-6); but we also heard him inform God that that he will continue his praise of women (47,1-8). In

Hausen's *'Mîn herze und mîn lîp diu wellent scheiden'* (MF 47,9) a crusader asks God to provide a warm welcome back home to his rebellious heart, even though it refuses its loyalty to God and crusader (47,27-28). We heard from the crusader in Reinmar der Alte's *'Des tages dô ich daz kriuze nam'* (MF 181,13) essentially the same expression of support for his similarly rebellious thoughts (181,33-37). In Albrecht von Johansdorf's *'Guote liute, holt die gâbe'* (MF 94,15) the crusader notifies God that a half-reward is due his beloved lady, even after having confessed (94,25-34) that his devotion to crusade duty is half-hearted and explicitly limited. And, to cite one final example, the crusader in Otto von Botenlauben's *'Waere Kristes lôn niht alsô süeze'* (KD 41 = KLD I,41,XII) similarly claims a share in his reward for his "heavenly" beloved ("mîn himelrîche," I,4), after admitting that he was very reluctant to leave her behind to seek Christ's reward.

Thus in both Latin and German poetry of the crusade, the (re)presentation of God is strikingly varied. Furthermore, the attitude expressed toward God encompasses in both a few cases of profound discomfort with God as the ultimate source of a troubling circumstance. In the Latin crusade poems after Hattin, the dominant concerns are the loss of Jerusalem and other (military) reversals of fortune; in the German poems portraying the crusader, the focus of concern is the pain of parting from home and, in some cases, from a beloved woman; in the German poems featuring the female persona, it is the loss of the beloved man inflicted upon the woman by the crusades.

Over against these manifold complaints, poems or even passages that merit the term propaganda or recruiting poems--which, as noted in our introduction, scholarship has tended to see as the dominant function of crusade poetry[165]--are strikingly rare. Even in the Latin crusade poetry of the period after 1187, works that clearly merit the designation propagandistic or recruiting poetry are not plentiful.

There may be good reasons why medieval crusade poetry expresses so much less aggression and martiality than modern scholars have expected or even claimed to find in these poems. For the idea of a Christian engaging in warfare at all, and particularly in the service of God, an idea with which representatives of the Church had wrestled intensely at least since Tertullian in the third century,[166] was still a virile source of conflict and discomfort in the age when the poems of this study were being composed.

Cowdrey points out that "right into the second half of the eleventh century, and therefore on the very eve of the First Crusade (1096-1101), the Christian West was teaching that killing or wounding in warfare, however legitimate the cause, was gravely sinful and merited severe penance."[167] Bishop Ivo of Chartres, a canonist who was active "just at the time when the first crusade was taking shape,"[168] and who was torn between loyalty to papal crusade policies and anti-war sentiment, admonished Count Hugo of Troyes that his marriage vows took precedence over his plans for crusade participation.[169] How Hehl can characterize Ivo's view on the crusade as "neutral"[170] is not clear to me. In any case, the crusading era began in an atmosphere of conflict and misgiving about Christian participation in warfare.

"The years from 1101 to 1187," in the words of Riley-Smith, "witnessed an extraordinarily ambitious fiasco and then a period in which the movement was at a low ebb in spite of activity in all theatres of war."[171] The ambitious fiasco in question was the Second Crusade (1147-1149), which ended in the devastating and humiliating defeat of the crusaders.[172] Gerhoch of Reichersberg and the Annalist of Würzburg, "the two severest critics of the crusade," subsequently went so far as to call this crusade "the work of the Devil and Antichrist."[173] The "low ebb" which Riley-Smith cites is pointedly illustrated by the pronounced reluctance of Pope Hadrian IV, ten years after the Second Crusade, to give his blessings to the wish of King Louis VII of France and King Henry II of England to launch a mission against the Moors in Spain.[174] According to Hehl, Hadrian hesitated mainly out of worry that such a mission, if not successful, could cause a repeat of the storm of criticism heaped upon the Second Crusade.[175]

And the severe criticism of the crusades on the part of Church affiliates found a new champion on the eve of the Third Crusade in the person of one Ralph Niger. Ralph Niger was a "twelfth-century English scholar, probably a cleric rather than a monk,"[176] who was an acquaintance of such clerical dignitaries as Sir Thomas Beckett, Archbishop of Canterbury, and John of Salisbury.[177] On the eve of the Third Crusade, probably around the turn of the year 1187/1188, Ralph Niger wrote a work entitled *De re militari et triplici via peregrinationis ierosolimitane*,[178] which Flahiff characterizes as "a systematic and well reasoned attempt to answer the question: *utrum peregrinandum sit.*"[179] The work becomes a strongly worded condemnation of crusading:

To go as far as he does at one point and conclude that one might
actually be interfering with God's designs by launching a crusade, is to
reverse completely the theme of the First Crusade.[180]

The arguments of Ralph Niger include the proclamation that God could
call up twelve legions of angels to fight for Him if it were called for.[181]
This idea of divine sufficiency without crusade violence sounds very
much like the one encountered in the poem 'Die hinnen varn' (MF
89,21) by Albrecht von Johansdorf. In the first stanza of that poem the
speaker rejects such an idea vehemently as "der tumben spot," that is,
as the scornful musings of shirkers who want to refuse God crusade
service. Apparently, then, this idea was in circulation in Johansdorf's
home territory of eastern Bavaria and western Austria.

In any case, Ralph Niger stands as the culmination of a
development, lasting several decades, in which notable representatives
of the clerical sphere exhibited a jaundiced view of a very difficult,
perilous, and costly involvement. How widespread this clerical
disenchantment was is difficult to tell. It has received very modest
scholarly attention. It is interesting to note that Niger's work received
no objections from his papal censor, the Archbishop of Reims.[182]

This high point of clerical criticism of the crusades coincides
very closely with the first known crusade poems in the German
vernacular. In these poems, as the present study has contended, the
crusades are criticized pointedly in some instances, praised very rarely,
and are targeted for almost constant complaining. Thus a statement
such as that by Patrick Murphy to the effect that "Whoever the antiwar
critics of the Crusades were, whoever caused there to be a debate, they
do not appear to have been the poets of the period,"[183] is questionable,
at least for medieval German crusade poets. One must, of course, be
cautious about trying to determine the personal stance of poets on the
basis of their poems. However, our readings of the German poems
suggest that their authors should not be too hastily excluded from the
ranks of Murphy's anonymous antiwar critics.

Similarly in need of rethinking is the statement of Colin
Morris to the effect that "Recruiting songs are rare until the third
crusade, and then there is a great outcrop of them, not to mention the
many Latin laments on the loss of Jerusalem."[184] According to our
readings, German poems meriting the designation recruiting songs are
very rare during the Third Crusade and beyond. Statements in favor of
the crusades do, of course, occur, sometimes as recruiting phraseology.
However, we found that such statements are few in number and tend to

occur in unusual contexts encompassing features which call into question their effectiveness as pro-crusade utterances. In fact, it would seem that many of the poems that we have encountered would actually have been more likely to discourage any potential recruits who may have heard them, rather than to arouse enthusiam and fervor. Certainly, it is difficult to understand how poems by Johansdorf, Hausen, and Reinmar--with their varied complaints about sinful attachment to woman, unwillingness to sacrifice love for her for the sake of the crusade, inability to commit decisively to the service of God--could have been useful for encouraging undecided or hesitant hearers to enlist. Oddly, however, it is a Latin poem, *'Ire si vis ad sermonem'* (KL 29) that is particularly direct and explicit in advising potential crusaders to firmly refuse attempts at recruitment.[185] The fact is that medieval German crusade poetry, far from being a propagandistic tool for swelling the crusading armies, is a poetry of complaints, of dilemmas, and of discomfort about an activity that was apparently disputed widely in both clerical and lay circles. From the little that we have heard about the circles in question, medieval German poetry fits into the picture very well as a set of statements which make their own contribution to the complex discussion of a very troubling issue.

Endnotes

[1] G(eorg) Wolfram, "Kreuzpredigt und Kreuzlied," *ZDA* 30 (1886):89. In the original, the statement in question reads as follows: "Die nachfolgenden untersuchungen wollen den nachweis führen, dass der inhalt der kreuzlieder des 12. und 13. jhs. fast völlig auf den kreuzpredigten und päpstlichen bullen dieser zeit beruht."

[2] Wolfram, "Kreuzpredigt" 97. In the original, the crucial passage reads: "In den deutschen kreuzliedern beschränkt sich der inhalt auf folgende grundgedanken:

  I. gott hat für uns gelitten.
  II. wir müssens ihm vergelten.
  III. auch unsere sünden fordern eine sühne.
  IV. wir erwerben durch unseren dienst die ewige seligkeit."

[3] Wolfram, "Kreuzpredigt" 95. The statement reads in the original as follows: "Bei Hausen sind die gedanken, die sich auf den kreuzzug beziehen, ganz in seine minnelieder eingeflochten und bieten wenig für unseren zweck verwerthares."

[4] Maria Böhmer, *Untersuchungen zur mittelhochdeutschen Kreuzzugslyrik* (Rome, 1968) 22.

[5] Böhmer, *Untersuchungen* 13 and 16-20.

[6] Böhmer, *Untersuchungen* 21. The passage in question reads in the original as follows: "Die Kritik an Gehalt und Realisierung der zugrundeliegenden Idee war wohl vorhanden, aber im Augenblick des ersten großangelegten Aufrufs an die Ritter--und ausschließlich an sie--war sie in ihrer Bedeutung sekundär (zumal sie die Idee, wenigstens in Deutschland, nie grundsätzlich bekämpfte)."

[7] Böhmer, *Untersuchungen* 20-21.

[8] Hermann Schindler, "Die Kreuzzüge in der altprovenzalischen und mittelhochdeutschen Lyrik," *Programm der Annenschule* (Realgymnasium zu Dresden-Altstadt (Dresden 1889) 1-49.

[9] Schindler, "Kreuzzüge," 21.

[10] Ursula Schulze, "Zur Frage des Realitätsbezuges bei Neidhart," *Österreichische Literatur zur Zeit der Babenberger*, ed. Alfred Ebenbauer, Fritz

Peter Knapp, and Ingrid Strasser (Vienna, 1977) 206.

[11]Schulze, "Zur Frage des Realitätsbezuges" 204.

[12]Schulze, "Zur Frage des Realitätsbezuges" 205.

[13]Schulze, "Zur Frage des Realitätsbezuges" 204.

[14]Peter Hölzle, *Die Kreuzzüge in der okzitanischen und deutschen Lyrik des 12. Jahrhunderts*, 2 vols. (Göppingen, 1980) 1: 9-14. Volume 2 of this two-volume set contains "Materialien," among them a few (Occitan) texts plus text summaries.

[15]Hölzle, Kreuzzüge 1: 12-13.

[16]Hölzle, Kreuzzüge 1: 101-103. His definition, with explicit exclusion of poems that do not fit it, reads in the original as follows: "Der Ausgrenzung solcher Gedichte dient die folgende Definition, die ausgehend von okzitanischer und deutscher höfischer Lyrik des 12. Jahrhunders die Kreuzlieder beider Literaturen als Poeme bestimmt, die in der Mehrzahl ihrer Strophen oder Verse mit direkten und/oder indirekten Appellen an ein Kollektiv der Wehrfähigen und/oder an einzelne Herrscher, z.T. auch mit dem Exempel der Kreuznahme eines oder mehrerer Herrscher oder eines Dichters oft in Parallele zur Kreuzpredigt zur Kreuzfahrt aufrufen."

[17]Hölzle, *Kreuzzüge* 1: 180 and 191.

[18]Hölzle, *Kreuzzüge* 1: 194.

[19]Hölzle, *Kreuzzüge* 1: 204. This particularly intriguing statement reads in the original as follows: "Alles in allem nimmt der vorbildliche Kreuzfahrer in den hier besprochenen Minneliedern geradezu irritierend distanzierte Haltungen zum Kreuzzug ein."

[20]Jonathan Riley-Smith, *The Crusades* (London, 1987) 41-43.

[21]Goswin Spreckelmeyer, *Mittellateinische Kreuzzugslieder*, Göppingen, 1987. Reprinted by permission of the publisher.

Hereafter the numbering form KL 1, KL 2, etc. will refer to this edition.

[22]Goswin Spreckelmeyer, *Das Kreuzzugslied des lateinischen Mittelalters*. München, 1974. Hereafter = Spreckelmeyer, *Kreuzzugslied*. I shall do my best to shield readers from possible confusion stemming from the differences in the numbering of the same texts in Spreckelmeyer's two books.

[23]Emperor Manuel I Komnenos, according to Spreckelmeyer, *Kreuzzugslied* 76.

[24]Spreckelmeyer, *Kreuzzugslied* 85, footnote 56.

[25]Unless otherwise indicated, the translations are mine, and are intended to convey the original as accurately as possible.

[26]Spreckelmeyer, *Kreuzzugslied* 91.

[27]Riley-Smith, *Crusades* 80 and 93.

[28] Spreckelmeyer, *Kreuzzugslied* 99f.

[29]Spreckelmeyer, *Kreuzzugslied* 103.

[30]Spreckelmeyer, *Kreuzzugslied* 111. The relevant sentence reads in the original as follows: "So wird für den Kreuzfahrer die völlige Hingabe im Glauben wichtiger als eine militärische Vorbereitung der Fahrt."

[31]Spreckelmeyer, *Kreuzzugslied* 239, 247, and 249.

[32]Spreckelmeyer, *Kreuzzugslied* 90, 197, 68, and 80, respectively.

[33]Spreckelmeyer, *Kreuzzugslied* 55. The statement in question reads: "Auf Grund dieser Spiritualisierung tritt der Kampf gegen die Heiden in den Hintergrund."

[34]Spreckelmeyer, *Kreuzzugslied* 257, 118, 141, and 84, respectively.

[35]Cf. Spreckelmeyer, *Kreuzzugslied* 267.

[36]Spreckelmeyer, *Kreuzzugslied* 58 and footnote 149. An English translation of St. Bernard's text from which Spreckelmeyer quotes in this footnote can be found in Louise and Jonathan Riley-Smith, The Crusades: Idea and Reality (London, 1981) 95.

[37]Spreckelmeyer, *Kreuzzugslied* 252. This phrase quoted here from Spreckelmeyer appears in Pope Eugene III's bull "Quantum praedecessores," which initiated the Second Crusade, in the formulation "nostris et ipsius populi peccatis exigentibus" to encompass the citizens of the captured city of Edessa and their sympathizers in Europe.

[38]Spreckelmeyer, *Kreuzzugslied* 238.

[39]Spreckelmeyer, *Kreuzzugslied* 248.

[40]Spreckelmeyer, *Kreuzzugslied* 145.

[41]See Spreckelmeyer, *Kreuzzugslied* 145-146.

[42]Spreckelmeyer, *Kreuzzugslied* 230 and 237.

[43]Spreckelmeyer, *Kreuzzugslied* 155 and 156.

[44]Spreckelmeyer, *Kreuzzugslied* 156.

[45]Spreckelmeyer, *Kreuzzugslied* 161.

[46]Spreckelmeyer, *Kreuzzugslied* 162-163.

[47]Spreckelmeyer, *Kreuzzugslied* 192; F.J.E. Raby, A History of Christian-Latin Poetry, 2nd ed. (Oxford, 1953) 273.

[48]Spreckelmeyer, *Kreuzzugslied* 81. I have not been able to locate a copy of Schmuck's *Mittellateinische Kreuzlieder*.

[49]*Mittellateinische Kreuzzugslieder* 41.

[50]Spreckelmeyer, *Kreuzzugslied* 131; cf. *Lexikon des Mittelalters*, ed. Robert Auty et al. 9 vols. (Munich and Zurich, 1989) 4: 1085.

[51]Spreckelmeyer, *Kreuzzugslied*, p. 257; *Lexikon des Mittelalters* (Munich, 1995) 7: 824-825.

[52]Spreckelmeyer, *Kreuzzugslied* 103 and 142-143.

[53]Spreckelmeyer, *Kreuzzugslied* 184.

[54]Spreckelmeyer, *Kreuzzugslied*, p. 225.

[55]Spreckelmeyer, *Kreuzzugslied* 54.

[56]Spreckelmeyer, *Kreuzzugslied* 55-58.

[57]Hans Jürgen Rieckenberg, "Leben und Stand des Minnesängers Friedrich von Hausen," *Archiv für Kulturgeschichte* 43 (1961): 169; D.G. Mowatt, *Friderich von Hûsen* (Cambridge, 1971) 18.

[58]Peter Weidisch, "Otto von Botenlauben," Otto von Botenlauben, ed. Peter

Weidisch (Würzburg, 1994) 24-26.

[59]Statements about German poets by later German poets, most of them eulogies, can be found in the anthology Günther Schweikle, ed. *Dichter über Dichter in mittelhochdeutscher Literatur*. Tübingen, 1970.

[60]Numbering with MF throughout the study will refer to vol. 1 of the text edition Hugo Moser and Helmut Tervooren, eds. *Des Minnesangs Frühling*, 36th ed., 2 vols. Stuttgart, 1977. Reprinted by permission of the publisher.

[61] For a discussion of the manuscripts in English, see Olive Sayce, The *Medieval German Lyrik* 1150-1300 (Oxford, 1982) 51-78.

[62] James A. Brundage, *Medieval Canon Law and the Crusader* (Madison, 1969) 116.

[63]The body clearly has that carnal role in the Klage-Büchlein of crusader poet Hartmann von Aue. See Leslie Seiffert, "On the Language of Sovereignty, Deference and Solidarity," in *Hartmann von Aue*, ed. Timothy McFarland and Silvia Ranawake (Göppingen, 1988) 21-51.

[64]Hugo Bekker, *Friedrich von Hausen* (Chapel Hill, 1977) 66.

[65]D.G. Mowatt, *Friderich von Hûsen* (Cambridge, 1971) 91; W.T.H. Jackson, "Contrast Imagery in the Poems of Friedrich von Hausen," *GR* 49 (1974): 15.

This metaphorical usage in which the heart remains with the beloved while the body goes elsewhere, which has impressed numerous Hausen-scholars as odd in the light of Christian traditional usage, is apparently also quite traditional in Arabic poetry. The opening line of a poem by the Cordovan poet Ibn Hazm (994-1064) included in the collection by Ibn Said al-Maghrib, published as *The Banners of the Champions* (Madison, 1989), reads in the translation of editors James A. Bellamy and Patricia Owen Steiner as follows:

> Though my body departs, my heart will stay
> with you always.

Other examples of this metaphorical separation of heart and body (in various combinations) can be found in Lawrence Ecker, *Arabischer, provenzalischer und deutscher Minnesang* (1934; Geneva, 1978) 56, 57, and 58.

[66]Hölzle, *Kreuzzüge* 1: 516-18.

[67]See Paul Salmon, "The Lyrics of Hartmann von Aue," *MLR* 66 (1971): 823; Volker Mertens, "Kritik am Kreuzzug Kaiser Heinrichs? Zu Hartmanns 3. Kreuzlied," *Staufer Zeit*, ed. Rüdiger Krohn, Bernd Thum, and Peter Wapnewski (Stuttgart, 1978) 329; Eberhard Nellmann, "Saladin und die Minne: Zu Hartmanns drittem Kreuzlied," *Philologie als Kulturwissenschaft*, ed. Ludger Grenzmann, Hubert Herkommer, and Dieter Wuttke (Göttingen, 1987) 143; Christoph Cormeau and Wilhelm Störmer, *Hartmann von Aue* (Munich, 1985) 94.

[68]Olive Sayce, *Romanisch beeinflußte Lieder des Minnesangs* (Göppingen, 1999) 19.

[69]Unless otherwise indicated, the translations throughout are mine, and are intended to convey the original as accurately as possible.

[70]Hugo Bekker, *Friedrich von Hausen* (Chapel Hill, 1977) 64.

[71] Sayce, *Romanisch beeinflußte Lieder des Minnesangs* 37.

[72] In MF, line 47,28 reads "an eine stât, dâ man dich welle enpfân; in KD, "an eine stat dâ man dich wol enpfâ." The line occurs in two manuscripts. In B, the Weingärtner Liederhandschrift (verse 11), the reading is "an aine stat da man dich wol enpfan," supposedly in the meaning 'to a place where one will (would) receive you.' This reading is very suspect since one would expect either *welle* or *wolte/wolde* as a singular form of the MHG verb *wellen*, (See Hermann Paul and Walther Mitzka, *Mittelhochdeutsche Grammatik*, 18th ed., Tübingen, 1959, 166, paragraph #173). In C, the Große Heidelberger (Manessische) Handschrift (verse 26), the reading is "an eine stat da man dich wol welle enpfan," which I translate 'to a place where one will/would receive you well.' The occurrence of the form "wol" in both manuscripts makes me suspect that they may both have modified a reading "an eine stat da man dich wol enpfâ" meaning "to a place where one may well receive you." The changes may conceivably have been triggered by editorial discomfort with the idea of a crusader praying for a warm reception for this sinful, obstinate heart.

[73]Bekker, *Friedrich von Hausen* 68.

[74]Spreckelmeyer, *Kreuzzugslied* 238-239.

[75]Mittellateinische *Kreuzzugsdichtung* 20.

[76]Spreckelmeyer, *Kreuzzugslied* 111.

[77]*Mittellateinische Kreuzzugsdichtung* 37.

[78]Spreckelmeyer, *Kreuzzugslied* 153.

[79]*Mittellateinische Kreuzzugsdichtung* 36.

[80]See Ekkehard Blattmann, *Die Lieder Hartmanns von Aue* (Berlin, 1968) 156; Christoph Cormeau and Wilhelm Störmer, *Hartmann von Aue* (Munich, 1985) 92.

[81]James A. Brundage in his *Medieval Canon Law and the Crusader* (Madison and London: U of Wisconsin P, 1969) makes no mention of a provision in canon law for a deceased person to share in the privileges of a crusader. And, interestingly, Hartmann's assertion in MF 211,20, that a faithful and supportive wife will share in her crusading husband's privilege, remained likewise without backing in canon law, according to my reading of Brundage (p. 154), until 1252, some half a decade after Hartmann's death.

[82]Spreckelmeyer, *Kreuzzugslied*, 111. Text: *Mittellateinische Kreuzzugslieder*, ed. Spreckelmeyer, 37-38.

[83]Cf. Blattmann 13-17; Paul Salmon, "The Underrated Lyrics of Hartmann von Aue," *MLR* 66 (1971) 811 and 823; Volker Mertens, "Kritik am Kreuzzug Kaiser Heinrichs?" *Staufer Zeit.* ed. Rüdiger Krohn et al. (Stuttgart, 1978) 325.

[84]Text with English translation in: Hartmann von Aue, *Gregorius The Good Sinner*, trans. Sheema Zeben Buehne (New York, 1966), 55 (lines 566-582), 68 (837-852), and 195-197 (3086-3131).

[85]Spreckelmeyer, *Kreuzzugslied* 113-114.

[86]E.g., Ekkehard Blattmann, *Die Lieder Hartmanns von Aue* (Berlin, 1968) 247; Volker Mertens, "Kritik am Kreuzzug Kaiser Heinrichs? Zu Hartmanns 3. Kreuzlied," *Stauferzeit*, ed. Rüdiger Krohn, Bernd Thum, and Peter Wapnewski (Stuttgart, 1978), 327-328; Hölzle, *Kreuzzüge* 1: 255; Christoph Cormeau and Wilhelm Störmer, *Hartmann von Aue* (Munich, 1985) 94; and Eberhard Nellmann, "Saladin und die Minne: Zu Hartmanns drittem Kreuzlied," *Philologie und Kulturwissenschaft*, ed. Ludger Grenzmann, Hubert Herkommer, and Dieter Wuttke (Göttingen, 1987) 139.

[87]Blattmann, *Lieder* 247.

[88]Concerning the influence of Hausen on Hartmann, see Leslie Seiffert, "Hartmann von Aue and his Lyric Poetry," *Oxford German Studies* 3 (1968): 21, and W.H. Jackson, *Chivalry in Twelfth-Century Germany: The Works of Hartmann von Aue* (Cambridge, 1994) 187.

[89]Concerning the importance of knighthood in Hartmann's crusade lyric, see Jackson, *Chivalry* 189-193.

[90] While Manuscripts B and C transmit three stanzas (=MF 88,29; 88,33; and 88,19, in that order!) in fair agreement with one another, Manuscript A transmits the first and third and a different second stanza under the name Niune. This second stanza also appears in C under Johansdorf's name, but at a different place in the manuscript sequence. Concerning these complexities, which do not effect our discussion, see David P. Sudermann, *The Minnelieder of Albrecht von Johansdorf* (Göppingen, 1976) 158-162.

[91]See Ulrich Fülleborn, "Kreuzzug und Minne in den Liedern Albrechts von Johansdorf," *Euphorion* 58 (1964): 340-342; Hölzle, *Kreuzzüge* 1: 231 and 510.

[92]In specific reference to KL 20, 'Miror cum tepeat,' but actually speaking generally of Latin crusade poetry after Hattin, Spreckelmeyer, *Kreuzlied* 252, says the following about this pat explanation for Christian reversals: "Die Erklärung aller Mißerfolge durch die Formel peccatis nostris exigentibus, wie sie meist lautet, ist in der Niederlage die notwendige Ergänzung zum siegesgewissen Schlachtruf Deus vult."

[93]Sudermann 185.

[94]Sudermann 185-186. In Hugo Bekker, *The Poetry of Albrecht von Johansdorf* (Leiden, 1978), the author makes a strenuous effort to get around the "sheer logic that 'minnen minnecliche' has an effect that is no less than selig-machend" (71). This effort includes an implausible translation: "des sünde wirt vor gote niht geseit" (88,35) is translated "about that no sin is spoken before God." Bekker's attempt to explain away the obvious is buttressed by a (mis)translation that is meaninglessly tortuous at best.

Hereafter, this book will be cited as Bekker, *Johansdorf*.

[95]Sudermann, *Minnelieder*, 241; cf. Hölzle, *Kreuzzüge* 1: 519.

[96]While C transmits four stanzas under Johansdorf's name, A attributes the same four stanzas to a Gedrut. In addition, Manuscript C also attributes the fourth

stanza at a different location to a Rubin v. Rvedegêr. Still, the scholarly consensus sees this poem as a creation of Johansdorf. Our findings agree with that consensus.

[97]Bekker, *Johansdorf* 90.

[98]Bekker, *Johansdorf* 90.

[99]Sudermann, *Johansdorf* 349.

[100]See William E. Jackson, "Das Kreuzzugsmotiv in Reinmars Lyrik," *GRM*, ns 43 (1993): 148.

[101]Marie-Luise Dittrich, "Reinmars Kreuzlied (181,13)," *Festschrift für Ludwig Wolff*, ed. Werner Schröder (Neumünster, 1962) 250. The passage in question reads as follows: "Sehr merkwürdig mutet die Aussageweise dem gote dem ich dâ dienen sol an (181,25). Ist es nicht ein ganz ferner, unpersönlicher Gott, von dem hier gesprochen wird? Ein irgendwie gearteter--unterstrichen durch den Artikel, der sonst für den Christengott nicht üblich ist--Gott, dem gegenüber es möglicherweise nur auferlegten Dienst (dienen sol), keine freiwillige Hingabefreudigkeit zu geben scheint?"

[102]Dittrich 250.

[103]Enno Bünz, "der Besitz Ottos von Botenlauben im Königreich Jerusalem," *Otto von Botenlauben* (as in footnote 101) 71.

[104]KLD = Carl von Kraus, ed. Deutsche Liederdichter des 13. Jahrhunderts, 2nd ed., 2 vols. (Tübingen, 1978) 1: 314 (Botenlauben is poet number 41; XII is the number of the poem). Reprinted by permission of the publisher.

This text, with German translation, can also be found in Jaehrling (footnote 103) 101.

KLD will refer hereafter to vol. I, which contains the texts of poems. KLD II is the commentary volume.

[105]Hans-Karl Schuchard, "Der Minnesänger Otto von Botenlauben," diss. U of Pennsylvania, 1940, 55 and 59; Joachim Kröll, "Otto von Botenlauben," *Archiv für Geschichte von Oberfranken* 40 (1960): 87-88; Klaus Dieter Jaehrling, *Die Lieder Ottos von Bodenlauben* (Hamburg, 1970) 2; Peter Weidisch, "Otto von Botenlauben," *Otto von Botenlauben*, ed. Peter Weidisch (Würzburg, 1994) 26.

[106]Jaehrling, *Bodenlouben* 109.

[107]Georg Drummer, "Otto von Botenlauben," *Bayerische Literaturgeschichte in ausgewählten Beispielen. Mittelalter*, ed. Eberhard Düninger and Dorothea Kiesselbach (Munich, 1965) 239; Dietrich Huschenbett, "Die Dichtung Ottos von Botenlauben," in *Otto von Botenlauben* (as in footnote 101) 223f.

[108]Carl von Kraus, ed. *Deutsche Liederdichter des 13. Jahrhunderts*, 2 vols. (Tübingen, 1978) 1: 314 (hereafter = KLD); cf. KD 60 (# 41) (with translation into Modern German).

[109]Erich Juethe, *Der Minnesänger Hiltbolt von Schwangau* (1913; Hildesheim, 1977) 2.

[110]Juethe 7 and 29.

[111]F(ranz) J(osef) Worstbrock, "Hiltbolt von Schwangau," *VL*[2] 4: 13.

[112]Juethe 6; Worstbrock 13.

[113]Juethe 4; Worstbrock 12.

[114]Hermann Menhardt, "Zur Lebensbeschreibung Heinrichs von Morungen," *ZDA* 70 (1933): 215-218; Carl Bützler, "Heinrich von Morungen," *ZDA* 79 (1942): 185; Helmut Tervooren, "Heinrich von Morungen," *VL²* 3: 805; and Hubert Heinen, "Heinrich von Morungen," *DMA* 6: 138.

[115]Juethe 18, 23, 47, and 54; Worstbrock 16.

[116]Gisela Kornrumpf, "Friedrich von Leiningen," *VL²* 2: 953.

[117] See Olive Sayce, *Medieval German Lyric* (Oxford, 1982) 39-43.

[118]Jonathan Riley-Smith, *The Crusades: A Short History* (London, 1987), 150, reports the following events (Frederick = Emperor Frederick II) from Brindisi and the surrounding area in Apulia from the year 1227:

> Frederick married Yolande (Isabella) of Jerusalem in Brindisi on 9 November and took the title of king of Jerusalem, having himself crowned in a special ceremony at Foggia. This led to the goal of his crusade being switched from Egypt to Jerusalem. Meanwhile quite heavy recruitment was occurring in Germany and England and by mid-summer 1227 large numbers of crusaders were assembling in southern Italy; they sailed from Brindisi in August and early September.

If the scholarly consensus that Friedrich von Leiningen participated in this crusade is correct--and I think this quotation enhances its plausibility--then we can imagine him being included among the large numbers of crusaders mentioned.

[119]Kornrumpf, "Friedrich von Leiningen" 953.

[120]*KLD* 2: 300-301; Karl-Heinz Schirmer, "Burggraf von Lienz," *VL²* 5: 825-826.

[121]See Olive Sayce, *The Medieval German Lyric* (Oxford, 1982) 272; Ioana Beloiu-Wehn, '*Der tageliet maneger gern sanc*' (Frankfurt, 1989) 192-194.

[122]The standard edition is *KLD* 1: 250-251.

[123] *KLD* 2:302.

[124] In the controversial fourth strophe of Hausen's '*Mîn herze und mîn lîp diu wellent scheiden*' (MF 47,9; KD 24), the speaker castigates the woman for behaving as if she did not understand his pleas and requests ("swie vil ich sî gevlêhte oder gebaete," 47,35). There is in this strophe no clear indication that the lady's behavior and the speaker's complaint have anything to do with the crusade. Indeed, there is nothing in this strophe to link it with the crusade theme, featuring the conflict between heart and body, treated in the other three strophes of the poem; hence the heated debates about whether this strophe should be viewed as a separate entity. For a thorough discussion of this issue, see D.G. Mowatt, *Friderich von Hûsen* (Cambridge, 1971) 60-81 and 94-95.

[125] See Adolf Waas, *Geschichte der Kreuzzüge*, 2 vols. (Freiburg, 1956), 1: 180-181 and 192; Elizabeth Siberry, *Criticism of the Crusades* (Oxford, 1985), 51,

101, 192, and 198; cf. Jonathan Riley-Smith, *The Crusades* (London, 1987), 104; cf. William E. Jackson, "Das Kreuzzugsmotiv in Reinmars Lyrik," *GRM* ns 43 (1993): 162-163.

[126] See Waas 1: 191-192; cf. Jonathan Riley-Smith, *The First Crusade and the Idea of Crusading* (London, 1986) 31-35.

[127] See Waas 1: 191-192.

[128] Friedrich-Wilhelm Wentzlaff-Eggebert, *Kreuzzugsdichtung des Mittelalters* (Berlin, 1960) 179.

[129] For a more thorough discussion, see William E. Jackson, "Poet, Woman, and Crusade," *Mediaevalia* 22 (1999): 265-289.

[130] J(ean)-M(arie) L(ucien) Déjeanne, ed. and trans. (into Modern French) *Poésies completes du troubadour Marcabru* (1909; New York, 1971) 3-5 (# I). KD 11 prints text with modern German translation. An English translation can be found in Frederick Gold, ed. and trans. *Lyrics of the Troubadours and Trouvères* (Garden City, 1973) 54-57.

[131] Mark N. Taylor, "The Lyrics of the Troubadour Marcabru: Vocabulary for Love as an Aid to Chronology," *NM* 94 (1993): 332.

[132] Ruth E. Harvey, *The troubadour Marcabru and love* (London: Westfield College, 1989) 177.

[133] Elisabeth Nissen, ed. *Les Chansons attribuées à Guiot de Dijon et Jocelin* (Paris, 1928; reprinted by Honoré Champion, 1981) 1-3 (# 1). Reprinted by permission of the publisher.

Concerning dating, see "Introduction" IXff. KD 22 provides text with modern German translation.

[134] Robert Lafont and Anatole Christian, *Nouvelle histoire de la littérature occitane*, 2 vols. (Paris, 1970) 1: 57.

[135] L.T. Topsfield, *Troubadours and Love* (Cambridge, 1975) 70.

[136] Cf. Harvey, *The troubadour Marcabru* 10; George D. Economou, "Marcabru, Love's Star Witness: For and Against," *Tenso* 1 (1991): 11-12.

[137] G. Muraille, "Guiot de Dijon," in *Le Moyen Age*, ed. Robert Bossuat et al., 8 vols. (Paris, 1964) 4: 362; cf. Nissen, "Introduction," XII; Robert Dragonetti, *La Technique poétique des trouvères* (Bruges, 1960) 320.

[138] Walter Blank, "Einführung," *Die kleine Heidelberger Liederhandschrift*, 2 vols. (Wiesbaden, 1972) 2: 126.

[139] Dejeanne XXXV; KD 10.

[140] James A. Brundage, "The Crusader's Wife: a Canonistic Quandary," *Studia Gratiana* 12 (1967): 435.

[141] Brundage, "The Crusader's Wife" 430-431.

[142] Helmut Tervooren and Hugo Moser, eds. *Des Minnesangs Frühling: Anmerkungen*, 30th ed. (Stuttgart, 1981) 437; Günther Schweikle, "Heinrich von Rugge," in *VL²* 3: 870.

[143] E.g., Ingrid Kasten, ed. *Deutsche Lyrik des frühen und hohen Mittelalters* (Frankfurt, 1995), S. 192, varies only slightly the punctuation used in MF and KD.

All three editions leave in tact the phrase "wande er revulte sîn gebot amme keiser Friderîche." The meaning according to this punctuation has God fulfilling his own command. In Kasten's edition, Margherita Kuhn translates the phrase in this sense: "denn er erfüllte sein Gesetz an Kaiser Friedrich" (p. 193). In the Kommentar, Kasten explains that God's self-fulfilled gebot is mortality, to which God sentenced man after the Fall: "Das gebot ist auf die Sterblichkeit zu beziehen, welche Gott nach dem Sündenfall über den Menschen verhängte" (p. 709). Thus God's self-fulfilled command (or law in Kuhn's translation) is for Kasten merely a complicated way of saying that Emperor Frederick has died (as a descendent of Adam).

For any who might find this explanation unsatisfactory, I would like to propose for consideration the following alternative. The lines in question could be punctuated as follows:

> nu wünschent algelîche
> Heiles umbe den richen got—
> wande er revulte sîn gebot—
> amme keiser Friderîche...

which would be translated:
Now let everyone wish
For salvation from Mighty God—
For he (= Friderick) fulfilled His command—
Because of Emperor Frederick...

Not only would this solve the problem (for me) of having God fulfill His own law, it would also provide a more satisfactory transition to the following lines in which the supplicants are told to pray that they may benefit from (spiritual) participation in the service of Emperor Frederick ("Daz wir geniezen müezen sîn," 97,13) and his fellow pilgrims, viz. by commemoration of Frederick's final godly acts.

[144] See Hölzle 1: 537.

[145] Hölzle 1: 546 notes the conflict with the preceding lines, but links the devil's scorn to the sleeping God pictured in the following lines.

[146] Hans Eberhard Mayer, ed. Idee und Wirklichkeit der Kreuzzüge (Germering, 1965) 14; English translation in: Louise and Jonathan Riley-Smith, eds. *The Crusades: Idea and reality* 1095-1274 (London, 1981) 57.

[147] See J.A. Burrow, *The Ages of Man* (Oxford, 1988) 107 and 162.

[148] Concerning the "Minnestrophe" of MF 102,1, see Hölzle 1: 561.

[149] Here I follow Hölzle in retaining the manuscript reading "liebes" which in our standard editions has been replaced by the conjecture "lîp" ('body').

[150] Hölzle's sensitive interpretation of the strophe (1: 560) reflects this lack of clarity on this point. He speaks of the personal commitment to crusade

involvement ("persönliches Bekenntnis zum Kreuzzugsenggement") in the strophe, but also notes that the speaker (whom Hölzle identifies with Rugge himself) argues exclusively on the metaphysical level ("ausschließlich metaphysisch argumentiert") and reveals no concrete connections with the reality of the crusades around him ("keinerlei Realitätsbezüge zur Kreuzzugsumwelt").

[151] Hölzle 1:561-562.

[152] Günther Schweikle, *Neidhart* (Stuttgart, 1990), "Vorwort" IX and 1. Franz-Josef Hofnagel, "Literarische Interessenbildung in der Neidhart-Überlieferung," *Interessenbildung im Mittelalter*, ed. Joachim Heinzle (Stuttgart and Weimar, 1993) 23.

[153] Eckehard Simon, *Neidhart von Reuental* (Boston, 1975) 17-20; Siegfried Beyschlag, "Riuwental und Nîthart," *Medium aevum deutsch*, ed. Dietrich Huschenbett et al. (Tübingen, 1979) 15-36; Hans-Dieter Mück, "Fiktiver Sänger Nîthart/Riuwental minus Fiktion = realer Dichter des Neidhart-Liedtyps?" *Neidhart von Reuental*, ed. Helmut Birkhan (Vienna, 1983) 74; Schweikle, *Neidhart* 54.

[154] SL = *Sommerlied* and refers to the edition Neidhart, *Die Lieder*, 3rd ed. by Hanns Fischer (Tübingen, 1968) 10-13. Reprinted by permission of the publisher.

[155] Ulrich Müller, "Die Kreuzfahrten der Neidharte," in *Neidhart von Reuental*, ed. Helmut Birkhan (Vienna, 1983) 95.

[156] See Karl Otto Conrady, "Neidhart von Reuental: Ez meiet hiewer aber als ê," *Die deutsche Lyrik*, ed. Benno von Wiese, 2 vols. (Düsseldorf, 1956) 1: 90-98; Olive Sayce, *The Medieval German Lyric* (Oxford, 1982), 39 and 229.

[157] Cf. George F. Jones, *Walther von der Vogelweide* (New York, 1968) 105.

[158] Ulrich Gaier, *Satire* (Tübingen, 1967) 11; Eckehard Simon, Neidhart von Reuental (Boston, 1975) 24; Siegfried Beyschlag, "Neidhart und die Neidhartianer," *VL*[2] 6: 873; Riley-Smith, *Crusades* 148f.

[159] See Siegfried Beyschlag, *Die Lieder Neidharts* (Darmstadt, 1975) 715-716.

[160] See, for example, Simon, *Neidhart* 22; Ingrid Bennewitz-Behr, *Original und Rezeption* (Göppingen, 1987): 205; Siegfried Beyschlag, "Neidhart und die Neidhartianer," *VL*[2] 6: 874.

[161] Gisela Kornrumpf, "Rubin," *VL*[2] 8: 294.

[162] KLD 2: 403.

[163] A fourth strophe in the same metrical scheme portrays a woman who struggles to answer the question whether it is right for a woman to accept service from three men ("diu dienest von drin mannen nimt"). In agreement with the scholarly concensus, I see this strophe as a separate poem. See KLD 2: 415, Gert Kaiser, *Beiträge zu den Liedern des Minnesängers Rubin* (Munich, 1969) 38; Kornrumpf, *VL*[2] 8:294.

Perhaps the strong divergence of this fourth strophe has protected stanza three from suspicion regarding its own divergence from the first two.

[164] See Kaiser 57ff.

[165] Cf. Colin Morris, "Propaganda for war: the dissemination of the crusading

ideal in the twelfth century," *Studies in Church History* 20 (1983):96.

[166] Louis J. Swift, *The Early Fathers on War and Military Service* (Wilmington, 1983) 38-47; John Driver, *How Christians Made Peace With War* (Scottdale and Kitchener, 1988) 31-35.

[167] H.E.J. Cowdrey, "The Genesis of the Crusades," *The Holy War*, ed. Thomas Patrick Murphy (Columbus, 1976) 17.

[168] James A. Brundage, "The Crusader's Wife," *Studia Gratiana* 12 (1967): 430.

[169] Ernst-Dieter Hehl, *Kirche und Krieg im 12. Jahrhundert* (Stuttgart, 1980) 10-12.

[170] Hehl 12.

[171] Riley-Smith, *Crusades* 107.

[172] Riley-Smith, *Crusades* 101-102.

[173] Hans Eberhard Mayer, *The Crusades*, trans. John Gillingham, 2nd ed. (New York, 1988) 105.

[174] Hehl, *Kirche und Krieg* 143.

[175] Hehl, *Kirche und Krieg* 145; cf. Christopher Tyerman, *The Invention of the Crusades* (Buffalo, 1998) 13.

[176] Siberry, *Criticism of Crusading* 1 and 41.

[177] Siberry, *Criticism of Crusading* 11; G.B. Flahiff, "Ralph Niger," *Mediaeval Studies* 2 (1940): 108.

[178] Ludwig Schmugge, *Radulfus Niger – 'De re militari via peregrinationis ierosolimitane'* (Berlin and New York, 1976) 16.

[179] George B. Flahiff, "Deus Non Vult: A Critic of the Third Crusade," *Mediaeval Studies* 9 (1947): 178.

[180] Flahiff, "Deus Non Vult" 179.

[181] Flahiff, "Deus Non Vult" 182; Schmugge, *Radulfus Niger* 196.

[182] Schmugge 62.

[183] Patrick Murphy, "Introduction," *The Holy War*, ed. Patrick Murphy (Columbus, 1976) 7.

[184] Colin Morris, "Propaganda for war," *Studies in Church History* 20 (1983) 96.

[185] Spreckelmeyer, *Kreuzzugslied* 181.

Bibliography

1. Manuscript Facsimiles

A = *Die Kleine Heidelberger Liederhandschrift: Cod. Pal. germ. 357 der Universität Heidelberg.* Ed. Walter Blank. 2 vols. Wiesbaden: Reichert, 1972.

B = *The Weingarten Manuscript.* 2 vols. London: Phaidon Press and New York: Praeger, 1969.

C – *Die Große Heidelberger "Manessische" Liederhandschrift.* Ed. Ulrich Müller. Litterae, Vol. 1. Göppingen: Kümmerle, 1971.

2. Primary Texts

Brunner, Horst, Ulrich Müller, and Franz Viktor Spechtler. *Walther von der Vogelweide: Die gesamte Überlieferung der Texte und Melodien.* Litterae 7. Göppingen: Kümmerle, 1977.

Dejeanne, J(ean)-M(arie)-L(ucien). Ed. and trans. *Poésies completes du troubadour Marcabru.* 1909. New York: Johnson, 1971.

Goldin, Frederick. Ed. and trans. *Lyrics of the Troubadours and Trouvères.* Garden City: Anchor, 1973.

Hartmann von Aue. *Gregorius: The Good Sinner.* Trans. Sheema Zeben Buehne. New York: Ungar, 1966.

Ibn Said al-Maghrib. *The Banners of the Champions.* Ed. James A. Bellamy and Patricia Owen Steiner. Madison: U of Wisconsin Pr, 1989.

Jaehrling, Klaus Dieter, ed. and commentator. *Die Lieder Ottos von Bodenlouben*. Geistes- und sozialwissenschaftliche Dissertationen 5. Hamburg: Lüdke, 1970.

Kasten, Ingrid, ed. *Deutsche Lyrik des frühen und hohen Mittelalters*. Bibliothek des Mittelalters 3. Frankfurt am Main: Deutscher Klassiker-Verlag, 1995.

Kraus, Carl von, ed. *Deutsche Liederdichter des 13. Jahrhunderts*. 2 vols. Tübingen: Niemeyer, 1978.

Kuhn, Hugo, ed. *Die Gedichte Walthers von der Vogelweide: Studienausgabe*. 13th ed. Berlin: de Gruyter, 1965.

Mayer, Hans Eberhard, ed. *Idee und Wirklichkeit der Kreuzzüge*. Germering: Stahlmann, 1965.

Moser, Hugo and Helmut Tervooren, eds. *Des Minnesangs Frühling*. 36th ed. 2 vols. Stuttgart: Hirzel, 1977.

Müller, Ulrich, ed. *Kreuzzugsdichtung*. 2nd ed. Tübingen: Niemeyer, 1979.

Neidhart. *Die Lieder*. Ed. Hanns Fischer. 3rd ed. Tübingen: Niemeyer, 1968.

Nicholson, Frank C. *Old German Love Songs*. Chicago: U of Chicago P, 1907.

Nissen, Elisabeth, ed. *Les Chansons attribuées à Guiot de Dijon et Jocelin*. Les Classiques Français du Moyen Age 59. Paris: Champion, 1928.

Riley-Smith, Louise and Jonathan, eds. *The Crusades: Idea and Reality*. London: Arnold, 1981.

Sayce, Olive, ed. *Romanisch beeinflußte Lieder des Minnesangs*. Göppinger Arbeiten zur Germanistik 664. Göppingen: Kümmerle, 1999.

Schmugge, Ludwig, ed. *Radulfus Niger: 'De re militari via peregrinationis ierosolimitane.'* Berlin: de Gruyter, 1976.

Schweikle, Günther, ed. *Dichter über Dichter in mittelhochdeutscher Literatur*. Tübingen: Niemeyer, 1970.

Spreckelmeyer, Goswin, ed. *Mittellateinische Kreuzzugslieder*. Göppingen: Kümmerle, 1987.

Walther von der Vogelweide. *Leich, Lieder, Sangsprüche*. Ed. Christoph Cormeau. 14th ed. Berlin and New York: de Gruyter, 1996.

2. Secondary Literature

Hugo Bekker. *The Poetry of Albrecht von Johansdorf.* Davis Medieval Texts and Studies 1. Leiden: Brill, 1978.

---, *Friedrich von Hausen.* Chapel Hill: UNC Pr, 1977.

Blattmann, Ekkehard. *Die Lieder Hartmanns von Aue.* PS & Q 44. Berlin: Schmidt, 1968.

Beloiu-Wehn, Ioana. *'Der tageliet maneger gern sanc': Das deutsche Tagelied des 13. Jahrhunderts.* Europäische Hochschulschriften, Series I: Deutsche Sprache und Literatur, vol. 1168. Frankfurt: Lang, 1989.

Bennewitz-Behr, Ingrid. *Original und Rezeption: Funktionsgeschichtliche Studien zur Neidhart-Sammlung R.* Göppinger Arbeiten zur Germanistik 437. Göppingen: Kümmerle, 1987.

Bergmann, Robert. "Untersuchungen zu den Liedern Albrechts von Johansdorf." Diss. U of Freiburg, 1963.

Beutin, Wolfgang. "'*im dienent Kristen juden unde heiden*': Das Gleichheitspostulat im Spruch L. 22,3." *Walther von der Vogelweide.* Ed. Hans-Dieter Mück. Stuttgart: Stöffler & Schütz, 1989. 299-314.

Beyschlag, Siegfried. "Neidhart und Neidhartianer." *VL²* 6:871-893.

---. "Riuwental und Nîthart." *Medium Aevum deutsch.* Ed. Dietrich Huschenbett et al. Tübingen: Niemeyer, 1979. 15-36.

Böhmer, Maria. *Untersuchungen zur mittelhochdeutschen Kreuzzugslyrik.* Rome: Bulzoni, 1968.

Boor, Helmut de. "Friedrich von Hausen: '*Min herze und mîn lîp.*'" *Die deutsche Lyrik.* Ed. Benno von Wiese. 2 vols. Düsseldorf: Bagel, 1956. 1: 35-42.

Brackert, Helmut. "Kristes bluomen. Zu Hartmanns Kreuzlied 209,25," *Liebe als Literatur.* Ed. Rüdiger Krohn. Munich: Beck, 1983. 11-23.

Brundage, James A. "The Crusader's Wife: A Canonistic Quandary." *Studia Gratiana* 12 (1967): 425-441.

---, *Medieval Canon Law and the Crusader.* Madison: U of Wisc P, 1969.

Brunner, Horst. "Bruder Wernher." *VL²* 10: 897-903.

Brunner, Horst et al. *Walther von der Vogelweide.* Munich: Beck, 1996.

Bumke, Joachim. *Mäzene im Mittelalter.* Munich: Beck, 1979.

Bünz, Enno. "Der Besitz Ottos von Botenlauben im Königreich Jerusalem." *Otto von Botenlauben.* Ed. Peter Weidisch. Würzburg: Schöningh, 1994. 71-88.

Brodt, Heinrich Peter. *Meister Sigeher.* 1913. Hildesheim: Olms, 1977.

Burdach, Konrad. *Walther von der Vogelweide.* Leipzig: Duncker & Humblot, 1900.

Clark, Susan L. "The Ill-Fated Search for Permanence: Hand, River, and Crusade in Walther 124,1." *Michigan German Studies* 2 (1976): 36-46.

Cormeau, Christoph and Wilhelm Störmer. *Hartmann von Aue.* Munich: Beck, 1985.

Cowdrey, H(erbert) E(dward) J(ohn). "The Genesis of the Crusades." *The Holy War.* Ed. Thomas Patrick Murphy. Columbus: OHSU P, 1976. 9-32.

Curschmann, Michael. "Waltherus cantor." *OGS* 6 (1971/1972): 5-17.

Dittrich, Marie-Luise. "Reinmars Kreuzlied (181,13)." *Festschrift für Ludwig Wolff.* Ed. Werner Schröder. Neumünster: Wachholtz, 1962. 241-264.

Driver, John. *How Christians Made Peace With War.* Scottdale, Pa.: Herald, 1988.

Drummer, Georg. "Otto von Botenlauben." *Bayerische Literatur-Geschichte in ausgewählten Beispielen: Mittelalter.* Ed. Eberhard Düninger and Dorothea Kiesselbach. Munich: Süd-Deutscher Verlag, 1965. 234-244.

Ecker, Lawrence. *Arabischer, provenzalischer, und deutscher Minnesang.* 1934. Geneva: Slatkin, 1978.

Economou, George D. "Marcabru, Love's Star Witness." *Tenso* 7 (1991): 23-39.

Eickhoff, Ekkehard. *Friedrich Barbarossa im Orient.* Tübingen: Wasmuth, 1977.

Flahiff, George B. "*Deus Non Vult*: A Critic of the Third Crusade." *Mediaeval Studies* 9 (1947): 162-188.

Fülleborn, Ulrich. "Die Motive Kreuzzug und Minne und das Gestaltungsprinzip in den Liedern Albrechts von Johansdorf." *Euphorion* 58 (1964): 337-374.

Gaier, Ulrich. *Satire.* Tübingen: Niemeyer, 1967.

Gallo, Ernest. *The 'Poetria Nova' and Its Sources in Early Rhetorical Doctrine.* The Hague and Paris: Mouton, 1971.

Glier, Ingeborg. "Meister Alexander (Der Wilde Alexander)." VL^2 1: 213-218.

Halbach, Kurt Herbert. *Walther von der Vogelweide.* 4th ed. Sammlung Metzler 40. Stuttgart: Metzler, 1983.

Haller, Rudolf. *Der Wilde Alexander.* Würzburg: Triltsch, 1935.

Harvey, Ruth E. *The Troubadour Marcabru and Love.* London: Westfield College, 1989.

Haustein, Jens. "Meister Sigeher." VL^2 8: 1234.

Heger, Hedwig. *Das Lebenszeugnis Walthers von der Vogelweide.* Vienna: Schendl, 1970.

Heinen, Hubert. "Heinrich von Morungen." *Dictionary of the Middle Ages.* Ed. Joseph R. Strayer. 13 vols. New York: Scribner. 6: 138-139.

Hehl, Ernst-Dieter. *Kirche und Krieg im 12. Jahrhundert.* Monographien zur Geschichte des Mittelalters 19. Stuttgart: Hiersemann, 1980.

Franz-Josef Hofnagel. "Literarische Interessenbildung in der Neidhart-Überlieferung." *Literarische Interessenbildung im Mittelalter.* Ed. Joachim Heinzle. Stuttgart: Metzler, 1993. 21-38.

Hölzle, Peter. *Die Kreuzzüge in der okzitanischen und deutschen Lyrik des 12. Jahrhunderts.* 2 vols. Göppingen: Kümmerle, 1980.

Jackson, William E. "Das Kreuzzugsmotiv in Reinmars Lyrik." *Germanisch-romanische Monatsschrift* ns 43 (1993): 144-166.

---, "Poet, Woman, and Crusade." *Mediaevalia* 22 (1999): 265-289.

---, *Reinmar's Women.* German Language and Literature Monographs 9. Amsterdam: Benjamins, 1981.

Jackson, William H. *Chivalry in Twelfth-Century German: The Works of Hartmann von Aue.* Arthurian Studies 34. Cambridge: Brewer, 1994.

Jackson, W(illiam) T(homas) H(enry). "Contrast Imagery in the Poems of Friedrich von Hausen." *Germanic Review* 49 (1974): 7-16.

Jones, Goerge F. *Walther von der Vogelweide.* Twayne's World Authors Series 46. New York: Twayne, 1968.

Juethe, Erich. *Der Minnesänger Hiltbolt von Schwangau.* 1913. Hildesheim: Olms, 1977.

Kaiser, Gert. *Beiträge zu den Liedern des Minnesängers Rubin.* Munich: Fink, 1969.

Kalinke, Marianne E. "Hartmann's *Gregorius*." *JEGP* 74 (1975): 486-501.

Kemper, Karl-Friedrich. "Zum Verständnis der Metapher *Kristes bluomen*." *ZDP* 90 (1971 Sonderheft): 123-133.

Kienast, Richard. *Hausens 'Scheltliet'(MF 47,33) und der Sumer von Triere*. Berlin: Akademie, 1961.

Kornrumpf, Gisela. "Friedrich von Leiningen." VL^2 2: 953.

---."Rubin." VL^2 8: 293-296.

Kröll, Joachim. "Otto von Botenlauben." *Archiv für Geschichte von Oberfranken* 40 (1960): 83-107.

Ladenthin, Volker. "Walthers Kreuzlied 76,22 vor dem Hintergrund mittelalterlicher Kreuzpredigten." *Euphorion* 77 (1983): 40-71.

Lafont, Robert and Anatole Christian. *Nouvelle histoire de la literature occitane*. 2 vols. Paris: Presses Universitaires de France, 1970.

Lexikon des Mittelalters. Ed. Robert Auty et al. 9 vols. Munich and Zurich: Artemis, 1977-98.

Madden, Thomas F. "Vows and Contracts in the Fourth Crusade." *The International History Review* 15 (1993): 441-468.

Martellotti, Anna. "Walther von der Vogelweide: *Nu alrest* (L. 14,38)." *Studi Germanici* ns 16 (1978): 5-39.

Mayer, Hans Eberhard. *The Crusades*. Trans. John Gillingham. 2nd ed. New York: Oxford, 1988.

McDonald, William C. "The Maiden in Hartmann's *Armen Heinrich*." *DVLG* 53 (1979): 35-48.

---,"Observations on the Language of Courtesy in the *Iwein* of Hartmann von Aue." *Interpreting Texts from the Middle Ages*. Ed. Ulrich Goebel and David Lee. Lewiston: Mellen, 1994. 219-256.

Menhardt, Hermann. "Zur Lebensbeschreibung Heinrichs von Morungen." *ZDP* 70 (1933): 209-234.

Mertens, Volker. "Der 'heiße Sommer' 1187 von Trier: Ein weiterer Erklärungsversuch zu Hausen MF 47,38." *ZDP* 95 (1976): 346-356.

Mertens, Volker. "Kritik am Kreuzzug Kaiser Heinrichs? Zu Hartmanns 3. Kreuzlied." *Staufer Zeit*. Ed. Rüdiger Krohn, Bernd Thum, and Peter Wapnewski. Stuttgart: Klett, 1978.

Morris, Colin. "Propaganda for War." *Studies in Church History*. 20 (1983): 79-102 (= Special Edition: *The Church and War*).

Mowatt, D.G. *Friderich von Hûsen*. Cambridge: Cambridge UP, 1971.

Mück, Hans-Dieter. "Fiktiver Sänger Nithart/Riuwental minus Fiktion = realer Dichter des Neidhart-Liedtyps?" *Neidhart von Reuental*. Ed. Helmut Birkhan. Vienna: Braumüller, 1983. 74-91.

Müller, Ulrich. "Friedrich von Hausen und der *Sumer von Triere* (MF 47,38)." *ZDP* 90 (1971 Sonderheft): 107-115.

---, "Die Kreuzfahrten der Neidharte." *Neidhart von Reuental*. Ed. Helmut Birkhan. Vienna: Braumüller, 1983. 92-128.

---, *Untersuchungen zur politischen Lyrik des Mittelalters*. Göppinger Arbeiten zur Germanistik 55/56. Göppingen: Kümmerle, 1974.

Munz, Peter. *Frederick Barbarossa*. Ithaca and London: Cornell UP, 1969.

Muraille, G(uy). "Guiot de Dijon." *Le Moyen Age*. Ed. Robert Bossuat et al. Vol. 4 of Dictionnaire des Lettres Françaises, Ed. Cardinal Georges Grente. Paris: Fayard, 1964. 363.

Murphy, Patrick, Ed. *The Holy War*. Columbus: OHS UP, 1976.

Nellmann, Eberhard. "Saladin und die Minne: Zu Hartmanns drittem Kreuzlied." *Philologie als Kulturwissenschaft*. Ed. Ludger Grenzmann, Hubert Herkommer, and Dieter Wuttke. Göttingen Vandenhoeck and Ruprecht, 1987.

---. "Walthers unzeitgemäßer Kreuzzugsappell." *ZDP* 98 (1979 Sonderheft): 22-60.

Newby, P(ercy) H(oward). *Saladin and His Times*. London: Faber and Faber, 1983.

Nix, Matthias. *Untersuchungen zur Funktion der politischen Spruchdichtung Walthers von der Vogelweide*. Göppinger Arbeiten zur Germanistik 592. Göppingen: Kümmerle, 1993.

Ohly, Walter. "Die heilsgeschichtliche Struktur der Epen Hartmanns von Aue." Diss. U of Berlin, 1958.

Paul, Hermann and Walter Mitzka. *Mittelhochdeutsche Grammatik*. 18th ed. Tübingen: Niemeyer, 1959.

Paule, Gabriela. *Der Tanhûser*. Stuttgart: Metzler and Poeschel, 1994.

Raby, F(rederic) J(ames) E(dward). *A History of Christian-Latin Poetry*. 2nd ed. Oxford: Clarendon, 1953.

Ranawake, Silvia. "Erec's *verligen* and the Sin of Sloth." *Hartmann von Aue*. Ed. Timothy McFarland and Silvia Ranawake. Göppinger Arbeiten zur Germanistik 486. Göppingen: Kümmerle, 1988.

Rieckenberg, Hans Jürgen. "Leben und Stand des Minnesängers Friedrich von Hausen." *Archiv für Kulturgeschichte* 43 (1961): 163-176.

Riley-Smith, Jonathan. *The Crusades*. London: Athlone, 1987.
---. *The First Crusade and the Idea of Crusading*. London: Athlone, 1986.
Ruh, Kurt, ed. *Die deutsche Literatur des Mittelalters: Verfasserlexicon*. 2nd ed. 10 vols. Berlin: de Gruyter, 1977-1999.
Salmen, Walter. *Der Spielmann*. Innsbrucker Beiträge zur Musikwissenschaft 8. Innsbruck: Helbling, 1983.
Salmon, Paul. "The Lyrics of Hartmann von Aue." *MLR* 66 (1971): 810-825.
Sayce, Olive. *Medieval German Lyric*. Oxford: Clarendon, 1982.
Schaefer, Joerg. *Walther von der Vogelweide*. Darmstadt: Wissenschaftliche Buchgesellschaft, 1972.
Schindler, Hermann. "Die Kreuzzüge in der altprovenzalischen und mittelhochdeutschen Lyrik." *Programm der Annenschule (Realgymnasium zu Dresden-Altstadt*. (Dresden 1889) 1-49.
Schirmer, Karl-Heinz. "Burggraf von Lienz." VL^2 5: 825-826.
Schmugge, Ludwig. "Über 'nationale' Vorurteile im Mittelalter." *Deutsches Archiv für Erforschung des Mittelalters* 38 (1982): 439-459.
Schuchard, Hans-Karl. "Der Minnesänger Otto von Botenlauben." Diss. U of Pennsylvania, 1940.
Schulze, Ursula. "Zur Frage des Realitätsbezuges bei Neidhart." *Österreichische Literatur zur Zeit der Babenberger*. Ed. Alfred Ebenbauer, Fritz Peter Knapp, and Ingrid Strasser. Vienna: Halosar, 1977. 274-295.
Schupp, Volker. *Septenar und Bauform*. Philologische Studien und Quellen 22. Berlin: Schmidt, 1964.
Schweikle, Günther. "Heinrich von Rugge." $VL^2$3: 869-874.
Schweikle, Günther. *Neidhart*. Sammlung Metzler 253. Stuttgart: Metzler, 1990.
Seiffert, Leslie. "Hartmann von Aue and His Lyric Poetry." *OGS* 3 (1968): 1-29.
---. "On the Language of Sovereignty, Deference, and Solidarity." *Hartmann von Aue*. Ed. Timothy McFarland and Silvia Ranawake. Göppingen: Kümmerle, 1988. 21-51.
Siberry, Elizabeth. *Criticism of the Crusades*. Oxford: Clarendon, 1985.
Simon, Eckehard. *Neidhart von Reuental*. Twayne's World Authors Series 364. Boston: Twayne, 1975.

Spreckelmeyer, Goswin. *Das Kreuzzugslied des lateinischen Mittelalters*. Munich: Fink, 1974.

Sudermann, David P. *The Minnelieder of Albrecht von Johansdorf*. Göppinger Arbeiten zur Germanistik 201. Göppingen: Kümmerle, 1976.

Swift, Louis J. *The Early Fathers on War and Military Service*. Wilmington: Glazier, 1983.

Swinburne, Hilda. "Walther von der Vogelweide and the Crusades." *MLR* 56 (1961): 349-353.

Taylor, Mark N "The Lyrics of the Troubadour Marcabru." *Neophilologische Mitteilungen* 94 (1993): 323-344.

Thomas, J(ohn) W(esley). *Tannhäuser: Poet and Legend*. Chapel Hill: UNC P, 1974.

Topsfield, L(eslie) T. *Troubadours and Love*. Cambridge: Cambridge UP, 1975.

Urbanek, Ferdinand. "Rhetorischer Disput im Dienste staufischer Politik." *DVLG* 67 (1993): 221-251.

Waas, Adolf. *Geschichte der Kreuzzüge*. 2 vols. Freiburg: Herder, 1956.

Wachinger, B(urghart). "Der Tannhäuser." *VL²* 9: 601-610.

Wagner, Norbert. "Die Lebenszeit des Wilden Alexander." *ZDA* 104 (1975): 338-344.

Wallner, Anton. "Zu Walther von der Vogelweide." *BGDSL* 33 (1908): 1-58.

Weidisch, Peter, ed. *Otto von Botenlauben*. Würzburg: Ferdinand Schöningh, 1994.

Wentzlaff-Eggebert, Friedrich-Wilhelm. *Kreuzzugsdichtung des Mittelalters*. Berlin: de Gruyter, 1969.

Wilmanns, W(ilhelm). *Walther von der Vogelweide*. 4th ed. by Victor Michels. 2 vols. Halle: Waisenhaus, 1924.

Wolfram, G(eorg), "Kreuzpredigt und Kreuzlied." *ZDA* 30 (1886): 89-132.

Worstbrock, F(ranz) J(osef) Worstbrock. "Hiltbolt von Schwangau." *VL²* 4: 12-17.

Index